D1373948

Culture Shock

Veteran's Guide to Adjustment

Omnisun Azali

ISBN 10: 1495390527
ISBN 13: 9781495390524
Library of Congress Control Number: 2014902431
CreateSpace Independent Publishing Platform
North Charleston, South Carolina

Table of Contents

Preface

Culture Shock: Veterans Guide to Adjustment was written for the military veteran from collective experiences and observations. The author observed not only the Iraq and Afghanistan coterie of combat veterans but also those veterans who supported combat missions. Furthermore, military veterans who only saw various garrisons throughout the nation and world are assisted by this book. The author found it an interesting discovery that many veterans who never found themselves in battle or war also experienced a rocky adjustment upon being discharged from the military.

This adjustment period is often deemed post traumatic stress disorder and sometimes that label is fitting. However, other times this adjustment process is simply the normal and expected growth period for veterans returning from deployment, discharging from the military, or both. In this self-help styled book, the veteran is given a hand up and encouragement by a fellow veteran. In Culture Shock, the author lays a foundation that has proved successful in his own adjustment and in the lives of other veterans.

With that said, I must thank the veterans who allowed me into their lives and gave me insight into their journey. Their names were not used in the text but their stories remain realistic and potent for the reader. It is worthy of note that it was my own judgment to exchange their names with random ones to protect their identity. Many of these courageous veterans spent hours explaining their adjustment process to me. And, in turn, I spent hours and weeks explain my own solution;

a step by step self-help solution that is detailed in this book. Sometimes we spoke over the phone and at other times we met at a coffee shop. All of them made this book possible. It was their stories in addition to my own that brought this text to life and gave it validity. It was the honing of this adjustment system, their stories, and their willingness to try my own methods that encouraged me to write this text. It must also be said that one good friend helped this book immensely by offering his deepest thoughts. It is not just that he is my dear friend and we served together in the Iraq War, but as this book was written, he was only a few months out of the military. He and others were the ones who I directed my initial adjustment plan towards. These veterans gave me support not simply with a pat on the back but they also ensured that my words and mentorship helped. They believed in this book as soon as I thought out loud about writing it. It was these close and old friends who fueled the fire in me to reach out to more veterans. So for that, I say thanks. And a special thanks to you "E".

It is also compelling for me to state that veterans are a special group. The general population should neither feel pity for them and nor should they ignore them. Veterans are capable leaders and society deserves to see the best of us. This book was written to bring the very best out of veterans returning to the general population so that veterans may continue to make contributions to society pass our military service.

I must thank my mother who always makes me smile. You are the best Sia. I will also thank my busy brother Yao, and my wife who reads my material in record time and who is sure to ask me questions from unique angles that further my own knowledge of the issue. A special thanks is given to researchers who, from a more technical perspective, helped shape this text.

And finally, an honorable mention and acknowledgement is paid to Chadrick Domino and all the other veterans who never had the opportunity to make the adjustment back into the general population. But as they say, old soldiers never die, they just fade away.

Sgt. Chadrick Domino, 1983 - 2007

1
Let's be Honest

Problems Rarely Improve By Avoidance

'If you don't know where you are going, you will wind up somewhere else'

−Yogi Berra

Culture Clash

Veterans trying to diagnose or typecast themselves with post trau-matic stress disorder (PTSD), or any other disorders, are limiting and stagnating their own post discharge life. In short, it is a practice to be avoided. Veterans should also be slow to accept the diagnosis of someone else; whether that person is a professional or not. Some issues that seem out of place and disturbing may be present through-out the general population. Though the issue may be magnified in the life of a veteran, it will usually be a cause of an adjustment period: from one culture to another.

An issue such as anger is often placed into the post traumatic stress disorder category. Many, both professional and onlooker, see anger as a telltale sign of mental anguish. They see this as a sign of more imbalances to come including violent behaviors. Anger can lead to violent behaviors in anyone and in any society, yet the anger of a veteran is usually a failure or an unwillingness to adjust back into the general population. It may also stem from the percep-tion that the general population neither appreciates nor cares to understand the veteran. Because of reasons of misunderstanding and a lack of tools for adjustment, many returning veterans with a spike in anger are deemed poor sufferers of post traumatic stress disorder.

Furthermore, oftentimes this spike in anger is directed toward the general population who do not share the same culture, norms, and history as those of the military grunts. This clash of cultures is at the root of something usually distinctly different than post traumatic stress disorder yet important in its own right. A waitress is unprofes-sional and unapologetic at a restaurant, a guy bumps into you on the street and does not even bother to turn around and acknowledge you. A veteran blowing up at these individuals may not be necessary, but it is not always connected to PTSD. Sure, the best sequence of events is to ignore the waitress' attitude and forget about the shoul-der bump on the street. Instead, veterans igniting in these situations represent a failure to adjust to the general population.

If we can, for a moment, imagine the situation of a young migrant family. We can, for instance, say that this family left worn torn Somalia and settled, finally, in Minneapolis, Minnesota. They, the Somalis, would struggle to understand not only the language but also the norms and cultures of their new society. And they will struggle more if they made no attempt to assimilate. The general population in Minneapolis, excluding the xenophobic folks, may also struggle in their attempts to understand these new people. It would be benefi-cial, in this scenario, for the Somalis to enter into some program for assimilation. And, too, it would be good for the general population to give them time to mature pass the initial culture shock.

Similarly with the above scenario, current and former grunts belong to a culture different from that of the general population. One may honestly ask, 'How could a military guy who comes from the general population now be alien to it?' The answer is quite simple. Life happens! The military career and other experiences shape the veteran's perception of life. This is reality is indeed true for all peo-ple, of all backgrounds throughout the world. A person's experiences change her throughout the years into the person she ultimately becomes. And the change is continual rather than stagnant. As the person changed significantly through experiences in his twenties, he will again change through experience in his thirties, and so on. Likewise, a 19 year old entering the military will see the world differ-ent after his enlistment. And, as this veteran leaves the military after 4 or so years, he is now part of another (military) culture: a hierarchal culture that conflicts, in certain areas, from the general population.

Behavior Changes and Labels

The change in behavior, as a cause of experiences, should not be resisted. When we resist the inevitable we ultimately find ourselves with higher levels of stress and displeasure. Rather than fighting or struggling against these changes, it is better to understand them and their implications. The severity within the adjustment period often varies from veteran to veteran. Sometimes the returning veteran simply has a different outlook on life with very little changes in his behavior. This is a veteran who is conscious of his thoughts and controls his behavior through self-discipline. However, this veteran may still have internal turmoil that he silently faces each and every day.

Other times, the veteran has a completely different behavior than the one he exhibited pre-enlistment. A different behavior upon re-entering the general population is usually seen as a cause for alarm by loved ones who secretly wish that you would return as the person that left. Many family and friends transform into expert psychiatrists and label returning veterans as "crazy", "shell shocked" or any number of titles that they have learned and now parity. These family and friends mean well. It would benefit them if they knew they were destroying instead of building the person they love. A loved one would be of greater assistance to the veteran by reading through this text and finding how the veteran could successfully assimilate.

Labels should be Corrected

Labels, boxes, and disorders are a hinder for veterans discharging from military ranks or redeploying from combat zones. These labels are sometimes said with genuine care, yet other times they are said either mockingly or in passing without much thought on the affects of the words. Too often, people insult others without thoroughly considering the other person's journey. Too many of us simply throw words at people when we do not completely understand the situation. But words have life, and continuously hearing that "you are crazy" may have ill effects on the veteran. Family members and friends should choose words wisely when speaking to veterans.

As a veteran, it is best to correct a protagonist the first time he steps out of bounds. If someone begins to label with shouts of crazy veteran or post traumatic stress disorder, stand up for yourself. Instead of attempting to exchange bellicose barbs with the protagonist, learn to lean the conversation into a respectful and safe zone. Jokes work well here and it also eases the potential for a serious argument or conflict. The veteran should remember that the verbal battler usually means little harm. They simple do not know how to tastefully joke or express themselves.

Nowadays, instead of crazy and shell shocked the new favorite label slipping from many tongues is post traumatic stress disorder. I do not want to reduce this phrase to conspiracy. There are veterans who suffer from this, and other mental disorders. However, while these definitions may fit for some, many other returning war veterans just need time and guidance on how to best adjust to the general population. This mentoring and learning approach is more important than the labeling and drugs associated with PTSD. This book guides the veteran with pragmatic and sensible steps through his adjustment.

Root of Behaviors and Thoughts

As stated above, the severity of a veteran's redeployment and post discharge adjustment issues may vary from person to person. Whatever the severity and whatever the type, it is important to tie your behavioral and adjustment issues and thoughts to a root. The root, or cause, of the change is important for adjusting back into the general population. Searching and finding the root of a thought or a behavior is completely necessary and it an unavoidable step in the adjustment process. Without the root of the issue, we battle and struggle with surface effects and not the causes. The effects are diversions from the issue, and the issue to be addressed is the root. The culture shock of re-entering the general population from the military presents itself with various issues. Thankfully, those pesky issues have roots of their own, and it is the roots that give veterans a way through their adjustment.

Military Connection or Not

Veterans who discharge and ask for compensation for any injuries during duty are often told whether the injury is service connected or not. This is the ultimate determination for all requests. Here too, in this self-help text, we ask the question of whether or not a behavior is service connected. The root of your issues may not have a military connection.

For many, there is convenience in blaming any and all weirdness and odd behavior on the military. Yet, many people simply have exhibited odd behavior prior to their military service. All veterans have known some grunts (for it could not be us) that seemingly have had anger issues from birth. This group came into the military with a chip on their shoulder and successfully maintained that chip until their military careers were over. Though the root of their issues pre-dates their enlistment, it may have been exacerbated by their experiences in uniform, as we shall see further below.

Other veterans have picked up behaviors during their military service that are unrelated to any of their previous duties. Partying and drinking, for some, may seem like cornerstones of the infantry way of life but it is not. Picking up alcoholism while in the military is not always connected to service. This vice could latch on to any college student or young adult. Though many times it, drinking drug abusing and partying, will be a genuine attempt to cope with stress, at other times it is the pitiful result of peer pressure. A young person coming into the infantry nearly always wishes for himself to be considered cool and part of the in-crowd. Therefore, he attends all of the infantry parties possible and drinks everything that he gets his hands on. Senior soldiers take advantage of his childish lack of sense by encouraging him to swallow up beer from bongs and take shots of liquor until he is incoherent. If our dear soldier here becomes an alcoholic, the cause was his need to establish and preserve his group status and not the military, or any official duties therein, itself. This peer pressure alcoholism, drug abusing, and partying is also seen outside of the infantry in many other military operational specialties.

Necessary is it to say that new recruits of the military branches must fit in. In these positions, one is not afforded the luxury of simply considering the military a job that you do for survival. Had this been the case brotherhood and exemplary esprit de corps could never be functionally established. Togetherness would be a theory and the units would be splintered. Therefore, the new recruit *should* try his best to adopt soldering and brotherhood into his own personal ethos but he should not reduce himself to an airhead. He should not subjugate himself to the terrible requests of senior soldiers to 'drink drink drink'. Instead, and under the pressure of the very ones he looks up to, he should use jokes to create a buffer zone between him and senseless mistakes. If this proves too difficult, he should find the senior soldiers who do not engage in partying and drinking, usually the best and most disciplined soldiers, and enter their coterie. From the above, it should be clear that both extremes are dangerous for new recruits: to fall head first into the trappings of military peer pressure and to isolate oneself as a means and measure for protection. Find balance.

However, as stated in the above, it should also be noted that the military may not have caused the problem but it may have worsened it. Issue to problem. Problem to crisis.

STORY – Introvert Reaches Extreme Normal

In this true story, we look at an army combat veteran who had been an introvert prior to his joining the army in 2004. In his native state of Californian he was anything but gregarious as he chose to avoid larger crowds and to spend the majority of his time indoors. This was not unlike many reserved young adults who shy away from society and take to video games. It could be observed that at this point he was able to be amongst crowds though he chose not to. He was a regular at the movie theater and enjoyed occasional dating. The point, if it escaped you, is that he was an introvert, but it did not hinder the quality of his life through his own perception. He was able to function as he well pleased. He was able to date and able to enjoy the company of friends as he so desired. He was not a misfit in his introverted ways. Instead, he was selective in how he spent his time and who he spent it with.

After six years of active duty and two long tours to Iraq, his behavior began to change drastically. The long time introvert became hermit-like. He holed himself in his apartment and cut ties with former close friends and certain family members. He rarely went out in public for non-essential reasons. For many of his former friends and family, seeing him in this state appeared to be bizarre, strange, and a cause for alarm. However, when one examines closer they will notice that this veteran displayed common traits of lesser degree his whole life. He was an introvert before and after his military service. The difference then was only an extreme of his previous normal. This extreme normal is often overlooked.

Though the extreme normal is overlooked by many individuals it is very important in solving issues by finding the root. Many veterans who deployed into warzones remember the prewar evaluation we were made to attend. Healthcare professionals took time to look at all of us (or at least they should have) and determined areas of concern. After our tour into combat and before we could enjoy a well-deserved stint of leave we were made to have a postwar evaluation. More healthcare professionals examined us, even closer at this occasion, and determined our wellbeing. They also determined our post deployment areas of concern with those of the pre deployment. This is a great way to locate the extreme normal in veterans.

This text goes further, below, in methods of solving the extreme normal and all other issues plaguing veterans today.

STORY end

Find the Incident

A veteran, experiencing either redeployment or post discharge behavioral changes, must find the incident responsible for his distress. Furthermore, if certain behaviors are deemed an extreme normal of what was previously present, the veteran must dig, still, deeper into his pre-military life. Yet for the veteran struggling with an extreme normal, balance may be his rally point. And, thus, he should too search for military events and incidents that caused imbalance in his life. For clarity and continuity of text, the extreme normal will no longer be explained separately. This case and the case created solely by one's military obligations will be presented together and in unison. When it is necessary for clarity they will be separated.

The incident in question may be multiple events, but it is usually one. One event. For combat veterans it may be represented by one brush with death among many. It could have been the zip of a bullet whizzing by your head in a hotly contested fire fight. For some, it is the scene of a fallen soldier as a result a battle.

For many, surprisingly, the incident causing turbulence will be an event without violence or the expected scenes of battle. Here, there may be neither gore nor brutality. For these veterans, the incident may be the intense heat of a Kuwaiti summer, the terrible guarantee of deployment mundaneness, or the continual chastisement of an insecure sergeant. Each of these three can alter behavior and affect a veteran's redeployment and post discharge adjustment into the general population.

Difficulty in Locating Incident will Vary

The event that caused significant changes to the veteran's wellbeing and behavior may prove easy to locate for many. This group usually replayed and relived that incident numerous of times. Some replay individual past events multiple times each day. These veterans may "redo" certain segments by changing the end or some other portion of the event. For this group of veterans, they do not need to search for an event because the event never left them. For a veteran, it can prove quite dangerous to stay in this position – of recalling former events automatically. This text shows exactly how these veterans can make the additional steps to recovery.

For others, they experience more difficulty in locating the incident that caused unwanted behaviors to creep into their lives. For these veterans, the causes of their negative changes were swept away into a metaphorical closet. They were put away yet they did not go away.

This was their way of 'healing' themselves; just ignore it. However, the effects of the incident often remain. To nullify the effects, one must find the cause. This method, of finding the incident related to negative change, is the only way to truly be productive in healing oneself.

This method is vital and unavoidable. It has been used, with the remainder of this text, to help dozens of veterans. It nearly always proves to be a very sensitive subject even when it seems as if it should not have altered the veteran's behavior. A parent, friend, or battle buddy could assist in pulling out details of these events to the benefit of the veteran. This friend should understand not only this section of the text but the entire book.

It should be said that many may believe that their change in behavior and thinking was caused by many events over a course of time. It is an understandable conclusion especially when stated by veterans of multiple deployments. Noticing these multiple deployment veterans over the years, one may see a consistent decline of acceptable behaviors and attitudes. From simple observation, one could state that it was the deployments that created the problem.

Some veterans voice out the same. Veterans who state clearly their unfitness for combat are sometimes given drugs for depression and pushed back into the direction of war. The veteran here will surely continue to suffer as a result of poor decisions by his leadership. However, even in this tragic yet true scenario there is usually a single incident that holds more significance than the others. There usually an event that stands above the rest. This text challenges the veteran to find that incident.

STORY – Veteran Recalls One Particular Event

In this story, we learn from a combat veteran redeploying into garrison and the general population. Upon his return, he experienced a shift in his normal behavior. One recurring theme was his nightmares that made a peaceful sleep impossible. This veteran, Steve, focused on everything but himself as he redeployed. He put his family first and chose to ignore himself.

When the methods of this text were highlighted before him, Steve stated, and correctly so, that he simply needed more time to calm down. What Steve did not understand was though time may cause improvement it is not a solution to the problem. The best solution is a plan that guides the veteran from a veteran's perspective.

Steve finally bought the logic and began to consider which incident was the main instigator in his path to adjustment. First, he recalled the many firefights he experienced during his tour of duties. He had participated in dozens of firefights as he engaged with an elusive enemy. Yet when he explained further, upon persistent requests, it was one incident that altered his attitude. There was one event among the multitude which he gave more significance.

The event he told was of an ambush during his first patrol in combat. He went further into gruesome detail. As two platoon members were gunned down next to him in a flash of a second, all of his training drifted away. Too afraid to shoot, he simply knelt behind cover. As the wounded platoon members screamed in agony, he laid there hoping for the battle to end. Though he would later mature into a seasoned soldier, this one event, above the others, followed him until he addressed it. The sense of cowardice followed him until he forgave himself.

As we go further into this text, we notice that recovery is not simply an identification of an incident and its calm replay. Recovery, and successful adjustment into the general population, is possible with the utilization of all the processes found in this text.

STORY end

Boxes and Labels

Boxes and labels are thrown at veterans from a plethora of angles and sources. Yet, it is the veteran's acceptance of these boxes that causes him to stumble. It is a chose to accept, deny, or ignore a box or label. It is important now that you step out of any and all boxes that you have stepped in or labels that you have been convinced of accepting. Whether the box label reads adjustment disorder or post traumatic stress disorder is insignificant at this point. Whether the title was given to you by a 'professional', an insensitive family member, or yourself is of little value. The goal is to set an objective barrier between yourself and the issues that you face.

It is smartly stated that one cannot think outside the box if he is standing in it. And, similarly, a veteran may not adjust sufficiently if he identifies with each label that comes his way. Be separate from issues, perceived problems, and troubles.

You are not Your Issues

For veterans, it is important to remember that they are not the nightmares, the flashbacks, hallucinations, or angry outbursts they experience. These are simply their experiences. Perhaps it would be better said that these are *some* of their experiences. With each experience there is an awesome opportunity to grow, learn, and teach. Each experience has the potential to add more than subtract from the greatness of our lives. Each experience develops a person through a myriad of ways, and this adjustment process is no different. It, the adjustment process, will contribute to the overall quality of the veteran's life. It will increase her empathy, abilities, and complete appreciation for life.

Once a veteran steps out of the boxes and away from the labels, she separates the problems and issues from herself. All of the titles that are generically attached to a box are no longer relevant. From this point, one begins to see all of her issues objectively. However, this is just the beginning. Those problems in that box cannot be ignored. There must be acknowledgment and not ignorance of current issues. How sweet it would be to take the box of problems and dump it in the ocean. How gratifying if we could grind up our issues and troubles into little pieces and spread them throughout the Sahara. Yet, we cannot place our problems in the closet, under the bed, in the Atlantic, or in a massive desert. Problems rarely improve by avoidance.

Acceptance first and success second. Outside and beyond the chains of boxes and labels and titles responsible veterans accept the issues that they must face. Jumping out of a box, does not suggest that veterans must ignore or turn away from pressing issues. Instead of success, ignoring an issue will ultimately lead to stagnation or a worsening of the problem. Many veterans find convenient ways to mask their issues. These troops place smiles on their faces or keep to themselves hoping time alone will heal their wounds. This is a common mistake as we saw in the above story. It should be remembered that there are many approaches to problem solving, but evasion is not one of them.

Summary

A veteran, in order to have a successful adjustment, must be honest with himself about his current issues. Finding the root of current issues, allows veterans to focus on causes and not effects. Without this most important step, veterans may experience a prolonged adjustment process. Whether the root is military originated or was worsened by your military service can change only the surface of the search. Regardless of its origin, find its root.

Step out of the box. It is much harder to think outside of the box when you are standing in it. It is also beneficial for the veteran to loose herself of labels. Once outside of the boxes and away from labels and titles, the veteran must not ignore his issues. Your issues must be solved. Avoidance and evasion is not an option.

The following chapter, *Meditation,* moves in unison with finding the root of the issue. Together with the other points in this text, they provide a path for veterans adjusting into the general population.

2
Meditation

Find Comfort In The Present Moment As You Block Internal Distractions

'Being aware of thought you are not thought'

– Mooji

'Take action in order to move toward your goals'

–Les Brown

Meditate and Heal

Practice of meditation has the ability to take thoughts from a subconscious or afterthought state to the surface where they may be addressed. Meditation is a vehicle, transporting thoughts, behaviors, and events from an oftentimes hectic and rambling swirl to an organized and clear image. Consistent practice of meditation has many uses. For a veteran adjusting back to the general population after redeployment or discharge, he will be excited by the effects of meditation. He may notice that meditation was the final (or missing) step in conquering anger bouts, anxiety, and stress. These issues, and others affecting veterans, begin and end in the mind. Therefore, meditation – which is a mental activity – is a pivotal step in the healing process.

Beginning and Breathing

In preparing for meditation, it is necessary to minimize the external distractions in your control. Televisions, computers, radios, and cell phones should be silent. Nearby loud people should be convinced to 'quiet it down' a bit. The noisy people and the pesky technology can all wait. This is your time.

Now that you have secured a quiet environment perfect for meditation, you can begin to relax. Appreciate the health that you do have. If it needs stating, your reading or listening to this text displays some positive health. You are not a vegetable. You have the ability to understand and comprehend. Furthermore, your reading or listening to this text displays your need to better yourself. This is not present in everyone. Some deny their issues and others recognize and ignore them simultaneously. Great start!

As you begin your meditation, draw in a deep breath. Concentrate on the breath and feel it move into your lungs. This method of breathing forces you to expand your chest as you pull oxygen within and causes you to become aware of your solar plexus upon breathing out. Some use this technique among many to move into a state of relaxation. The practice of deep breathing has the potential to reduce stress and fits of anger. Others use an equally simple method of counting; whether forward or backward. These *counters* may calmly whisper each number from 10 to 1 or, if really under pressure, from 20 or more to 1. There is no wonder why many anger management courses and groups teach some system of counting as a means to counter unwanted rage.

As you become relaxed, become thankful for your gifts, abilities, health, and sanity. Acknowledge yourself. One element that should not avoid notice is your journey: from where you came to who you are. Each experience along that journey carved you into the unique piece of art that you are today. Breathing deeply or counting from 1 to 20 are excellent methods for enter into meditation. However, after silencing nearby noise factors and counting to 100, there are still other hindrances to this practice. These are internal distractions.

Internal Distractions

Internal distractions may also be called internal disturbances. These disturbances, if left unattended, reduce meditation to a pathetic monologue. They keep our internal environment from complete peace. Since these distractions have the power to derail meditation and consequently discourage its practice, we will now give them focus.

Internal distractions are represented by thoughts of fleeting things and old pesky issues. Internal distractions, by definition, move around uncontrollably and are most notable when we sit for quiet time or during the practice of meditation. These thoughts swirl around and create a poor environment for meditation.

This particular struggle for internal tranquility is the pressing issue for many veterans as they begin the practice of meditation. As the veteran meditates further, she will find that reducing this internal noise is a simple task. This collective noise the veteran experiences during meditation may represent things in the distant past, the near past, an agenda list, or various anxieties.

An interesting characteristic of internal distractions are that they usually rise and fall at their own pace. This is, of course, if they are allowed to rant and bark. Here we see the practice of meditation involving determination. Determination, or will power, is necessary in every corner of life. It was necessary during deployment, during garrison, and during discharge. It is also of great importance during the practice of meditation. A veteran must use determination to quiet these thoughts. Remember why you are here and stay focused.

A helpful method for lessening internal distractions is to, again, whisper a countdown from 10 to 1; or 100 to 1. Repeat this as many times as necessary. You will find that the numbers take the positions of the other disturbingly random thoughts. As the thoughts lose power and disappear, notice them one by one. Here, the veteran must be careful not to give too much attention to these automatic and fleeting thoughts. Instead, one should give each malignant thought a small and gentle acknowledgment minus any analysis. The veteran must see them at face value and avoid digging too deep.

As an example of the above, a catchy pop song repeating in your head during meditation and quiet time is only that: a catchy pop song void of meaning. With this scenario, it is not necessary for a veteran, at this stage in the practice of her meditation, to analyze when she first heard this song, why this particular song is looping continuously in her mind instead of another, and the underlying message of the song. Neither should this veteran try to determine the meaning of the snippet being repeated or the overall significance of this particular song repeating at this particular time. Instead, she must simply notice the song and wave bye to it. If acknowledging the thoughts without analyzing becomes tricky, simply ignore the thought completely as it fades away.

It should be stated, parenthetically, that there *is* a difference with the above two methods. When noticing thoughts during meditation, you become increasingly aware of the subjects of your mind; and consequently, of that which your mind is made. Humor may even ensue as you notice a pesky thought's attempt to enter then reenter your mind during meditation. When we choose not to notice unpermitted thoughts we steer clear of the unfortunate side effect of total derailment of our meditation. This derailment is caused, in part, by complete attention to the meaningless. As a veteran concentrates on a thought that irrupted in meditation, he will notice, oftentimes, that the meditation has taken a backseat to the out of place thought. Veterans must decide through practice of both methods whether or not to notice each fleeting thought during meditation.

The above could be paraphrased by the following statement: a veteran must find comfort in the present moment while blocking internal distractions. The nature of these disturbing distractions will most usually be either a replay of a past event or a scenario in the future. It is also quite normal and expected that these distractions will have a negative or depressing theme.

Unfortunately, many people remember an insult hurled at them much sooner than the warm smile of a stranger. Most people are flattered easy and offended easily. Meditation assists our will power to no longer fight insults but rather automatic emotions. The scenarios set in the future are many times better suited for a drama filled motion picture. Too many of these fantasy dramas place a person in either a depressing situation or in the false light of greedy conquest. For a veteran redeploying from combat or discharging from active duty, he must silence internal distraction whether they are a past event or a future scenario.

Organizing Your Thoughts

It is important that each veteran give meditation time to grow and develop. The distractions, once located, are not always easy to silence. Persistent practice of meditation builds a wall against malignant thoughts. Some of these thoughts leave consciousness only to sneak back into the mind after a few moments. Others of these leave completely and are simultaneously replaced by another out-of-control thought; as if they are renting the space of your mind. This chase may frustrate many veterans; yet, the purpose of meditation is being accomplished. Through the silencing of meaningless thoughts and fears the veteran shifts her consciousness and becomes increasingly aware of her thoughts. The veteran, at this point in meditation, is seeing thoughts that are, and have been, out-of-control. Previous to persistent meditation these malign thoughts were sporadic and ignored; now they are sporadic and seen. As the veteran continues to practice meditation these thoughts will further lose their power to disturb and stray.

The mind of most veterans, prior to meditation, consisted of uncontrolled and unmaintained thoughts swirling through their heads. This phenomenon meant that various random thoughts moved through the consciousness of the veteran while driving, while working, and even while reading. This is the undeclared norm for too many. Though a veteran practicing meditation may not have totally silenced and controlled these feral thoughts, it *is* an accomplishment that he is now aware of them. That alone is a great step.

Meditation and Boredom

For many veterans, meditation will seem, at first glance, painstakingly boring. Many will lift up their voices and cry out that the practice is simply not stimulating enough. Onward, they might ask 'Why am I doing this?' or 'Why am I sitting on a chair all alone?' Many veterans may, as a result of this particular boredom, question the utility of meditation.

Certainly, meditation should not bore. Most potentially, it is formed (of whatever quality) by the person meditating. Therefore, it becomes as exciting or as boring as the veteran creates. A great tool for lessening the perceived burden of boredom is persistence. The practice of meditation nearly always becomes stronger with regular sessions. Through time, meditation will not cause boredom to creep into your mind (if this was ever the case).

Along with persistence in practice, the veteran must use meditation to gather and organize her thoughts and critically focus on her character. As stated in the above text, meditation is *not* simply quite time. It is a time tested tool for edification and comfort. A veteran using pointed focus to give her meditation purpose will experience greater benefit and enjoyment than the veteran who sits imagining an upcoming television program or some revenge that will not escape him next time. A veteran must, as a rule, exist in the moment of meditation. She must know, concretely, that the practice of meditation is not simply an auxiliary activity. It, this practice, is one of the foundational activities for a veteran after redeployment or discharge. The preceding sentence alone should dispel all thoughts of insipidity within meditation.

Consistency is Key

Consistency and persistence are – collectively – the major key to a veteran's successful practice of meditation. Practice and repetition build the veteran's meditational strength. As a result of consistency those internal distractions will fade quicker. That repetitive catchy song will disappear with greater ease as you practice. Uncontrollable external distractions will have less of an effect as you make medi-tation a habit. Car horns, sirens, and loud neighbors may all irritate, distract, and disturb at first, yet eventually these noisy occurrences will have little effect. Soon, their power to irritate will fade away like those internal distractions.

An important decision for consistency in this practice is to allot a specific time for meditation. One hour twice a day is monk-like. Over time, the veteran may find his meditation schedule expand-ing. However, at this early stage schedule a 10 minute meditation for each morning. This may seem simple, and for many it will be, yet others may follow this schedule only for a few days then give it up. For that group, it is important that they remember consistency and persistence are key. Other times, the 10 minute session goes on for longer as the veteran's awareness shifts from time to meditation.

A veteran should avoid keeping time with some form of alarm. These devises cause significant disturbances to meditation. Instead, keep time on a watch or a wall clock. With this method, a veteran whom continues meditation past the designated time is not pushed out of focus.

Unmanly

As with many population segments, there are some veterans whom shy away or avoid meditation. These among our coterie are less enthu-siastic about following a meditation schedule than others. There are many individualized reasons for why they are less than inspired to sit in silence. Some of those reasons, as mentioned in the text above, are that they find it disengaging and boring. Others consider it a poor use of 10 minutes and proclaim further that there are more important things to do with their mornings. Further, there are veterans whom wholeheartedly believe the practice of meditation will have little to no positive affect. For these persons above, they must show determination to create the smoothest adjustment into the general population as possible.

There is, one, recurring excuse with few men that stands between they and successful meditation. This bunch perceives the practice of meditation as feminine. As they deem it lady like to sit in silence while considering their thoughts, they subconsciously block any and all good from the practice. It must be stated, for these veterans, that meditation is as manly as it gets!

It could be reasonably said that men, from various geographical locations, wish to know themselves and their thoughts. It could also be claimed that they, normally, focus on self-improvement. These are general viewpoints that many men hold and accept. Conveniently there is meditation, which accomplishes all of the above simultaneously. In addition to its supportive role as self-seeker, meditation also alleviates stress, anxiety, depression, nightmares, and flashbacks. Meditation is an androgynous tool in placing your life back on balance. It is an essential element during adjustment. Along with the other points in this book, the practice of meditation calmly and gently places veterans into the general population.

Goal Setting

Goal setting is a pivotal meditation activity. Veterans whom have silenced both internal and external distractions will find it time to begin this life altering practice. A worthy use for meditation is to establish and detail your goals.

Veterans should set and create goals which are private, large, and obtainable. A goal to have a family barbeque on a weekend is a great idea but it is simply not large enough; it is not challenging enough. Likewise, a goal to learn eight additional languages within a year is unobtainable for all but a few. I salute you if you are part of those linguists. A final step in creating and striving toward a goal is to keep it private. Maintaining privacy is not a subterfuge. The difference here is intention. A veteran keeps his closest desires, wishes, and goals to himself to redirect misguided focus into obtaining that goal. Exchange time spent spreading wishes for time spent practicing meditation. As these three criteria for goal setting are combined, the veteran will elevate in both meditation and life.

Goals and Milestones

A veteran should also consider a fourth criterion when setting a goal, which is assuring it is of her interest. The goal, if worthy and proper, is a thing that you excel at or have always wanted to be involved with. Time spent in meditation is great for grasping interests and setting goals. Most usually, the goal which you are searching for is right under your nose. The previous sentence, though wrapped in a tired cliché, is perhaps better explained that the goal you are in search of must not struggle or conflict with who you currently are. Goals require attention and interest; without out these it will likely founder. Instead of a struggle, selected goals should be an idea that you have played with for some time and now, naturally, are ready to put into fruition.

A veteran must use meditation in finding not only the large and obtainable goal but also the milestones that will accompany it. As a veteran employs significant and key milestones, she will not astray from her goals. She will continuously find herself aligned with any goal she has conceived. A milestone is a smaller target that points towards the direction of a goal. If your goal is to take the final leap in becoming a professional pugilist, your milestones may be to find a suitable gym and trainer, purchase the necessary boxing equipment, and lose the excess pounds so you are within your weight limit. All of these milestones will lead smoothly into the goal: stepping your feet in the ring on fight night. Remember, goals come in a variety of types.

STORY – A Lawyer in Training

During the original drafting of this text, a veteran named Jorge shared his goal of becoming a lawyer. It was, and still is, a noble and suitable goal. It is reachable, practical, realistic, and meaningful. It is also large enough to have an impact on this veteran's life. However, the road to success was rocky and filled with doubt.

First, Jorge questioned himself out of the goal that he himself created. This is the scenario for too many. Unfortunately, it is too often that we simply talk ourselves out of our goals and plans. If they seem impractical or farfetched, we simply bury them somewhere never to be seen again. It is the convenient way to avoid effort and possible failure. Another helpful benefit of meditation for veterans is the removal of the fear of failure. All things are possible. Jorge's story, continued below, shows the difference that confidence made in his life.

"I can't be a lawyer," Jorge stated while explaining the last few months of his life. "I have a career, a wife, three kids, and a terminally ill mother to take care of. I just don't have the time." It is a pitiful fact that each person is usually his biggest obstacle. Jorge piled on the excuses to avoid even starting out on the road to becoming a lawyer. As an example of automatic conditioning, he was attempting to protect himself from any distant failure. In essence, he was limiting himself for whatever embarrassment that could come.

Jorge, a navy veteran of 12 years and several deployments, was in his late thirties and battling an occasional temper as he adjusted to the general population. As he began to look through the points contained in the chapter of this book, he began to meditate. As created a consistent and persistent habit of this practice, he once again fell in love with this distant goal of studying law. At this time, Jorge, remembered all the reasons why he wanted to become a lawyer and what he would do with that law degree. It is interesting to note that his interests never shifted throughout this time. Instead, it was only his attention in this interest that wavered. Lack of interest combined with a lack of confidence hammered his goal into the ground before it had a chance to blossom.

Through meditation and will power, Jorge began to change the negatives of his life into positives. His statements explaining inability transformed into affirmations of possibility. Though Jorge had yet to earn a bachelor's degree and despite standing within reach of 40 he began putting his goal in place. He made provisions to get where he belonged. Jorge placed his self-limiting and strangling excuses to the side and completed his bachelor's degree in night school. More encouraging, he accomplished this while taking care of his ill mother and his family of five. Further, he graduated while working more than nine hours a day. This is the power of self-determination!

Jorge is currently enrolled in a respected law school in California.

STORY end

Goals help veterans charge forward with a purpose. It is goal setting that continues to challenge troops beyond enlistment. Some veterans may notice themselves, post discharge and after redeployment, floating throughout life without direction. This must be avoided. Goals, spurring us with ambition, fill in the spaces and gaps of our life.

Summary

The practice of meditation is an important and key component when veterans make their adjustment into the general population. Whether adjusting after war or after garrison, meditation allows veterans to know the deepest thoughts of their mind. This practice allows them to engage in intimate time with their own self.

Meditation is also a great tool for staying balanced once you have achieved that adjustment. It is not, by any standard, a temporary tool for adjustment. It is a practice that, once learned and experienced, will always stand with the veteran.

The external and internal distractions can come like a tidal wave. It is best to silence all of the external distractions that are in your control and focus on silencing the internal thoughts that run out-of-control. External distractions, including people and cars, are not always in the control of the meditator. Yet as the veteran continues to develop this practice, these distractions will cause less of a disturbance. Internal distractions are the fleeting and meaningless thoughts that can potentially derail meditation. The methods of quieting these incoherent rambles and thus reducing their power are described in the text above. These methods will ensure a meditation session free of mind created distractions.

It is important that each veteran bring meditation into their schedule. Consistency and persistence are fundamental in creating better meditation sessions. 10 minutes of meditation each morning is a great start. As you begin meditating, you will find yourself stretching the time gradually and naturally.

Each veteran must begin goal setting. Goals should be large, obtainable, and private. Goals challenge and spur growth and development. Keeping goals private allows them to flourish without external pressure. Many veterans may struggle to grab a goal, but worthy goals are usually hidden in plain sight. It is good to remember that goals are of current interest to the veteran even if he gives it little attention. Find the goal, become dedicated in obtaining it, and start employing milestones to keep you on track. These goals fill us with ambition each and every day and are building blocks for adjustment into the general population.

3
Reflection

Each Event Is Purely What You Perceive It To Be

'Every problem is a gift - without problems we would not grow'

– Tony Robbins

Begin Reflecting

Use silent time and mediation to begin reflecting on past events. Choose a wide range of events of seemingly various importance. The events may be from childhood or warfare. Bring each event, separately, into your attention. Using a wide range of events allows us to analyze areas that we may normally ignore; areas that may have been instrumental in creating the person that we currently are.

When we reflect, we especially remember the bad. However, we must put forth a determined effort to remember the good as well. For many combat veterans, it is quite easy to remember their first firefight, a roadside bomb followed by an ambush, or a mortar bombardment and the alarm sirens blaring for all to here. Those events will play on queue in the veterans mind. With will we can also remember the humbling moments of life. We will remember training sessions in the military; times when we learned brotherhood and wellness. We will remember the humorous times as we endured our training rigors next to other worthy grunts. And beyond the military, we remember our childhood and pre-military years. We remember and reflect on it all.

Emotional Events

Certain charged events can replay on demand or automatically within the mind for any number of reasons. One very important reason, which is at the background of most others, is the amount of emotion that is tied to these events; such as the emotion of seeing a good friend suddenly wounded by the enemy. The emotion here is not easily washed away even when it would serve us best to do so. Also, many veterans, and people in general, seem to enjoy attaching themselves to a sad story. For some, a sad story adds character to their personality. It is very important for veterans to elevate above this line of thought. A veteran's story creates his personality and character. That story must not necessarily be filled with drama and despair. A handshake from the principal of a high school as a young graduate walks across the stage also shapes the character. See as much as possible.

Another reason these events are easily recalled is not only the emotion wrapped around them but also the attention that many veterans give them. Because of this combination of emotion associated with an event and the attention paid to an event it is harder to remember a friendly gesture than a near death experience. Close quarter combat with the enemy dwarfs eating lunch from a Meals Ready to Eat bag with your battle buddies in the smoldering heat of the Middle East.

Labeling and Comparing

Once you begin reflecting on an event, remind yourself not to compare and contrast. See the event not in the light of another event but as a standalone event on its own. Avoid comparing the past event not only with other past events but also with the current situation of your life. The most functional use of reflection is to see an event objectively and not to tread the slippery slope of comparing and contrasting.

Similar is the case with labeling. Labeling comes natural to many people; events are good, bad, moral, unethical, cold hearted, loving, sociopathic, respectful, psychopathic, spiteful and so much more. One label is all it takes to step back into a box. In the first chapter we discussed understanding your current position without the limitations and expectations of a box. In this way, we give ourselves room to grow and deal with the issues at hand. It is a much better approach than simply providing a rushed synopsis of a complex situation. Many professionals have provided boxes and labels that have acted as self-fulfilling prophesies for veterans simply making an adjustment. Post Traumatic Stress Disorder is a box that is fitting for some veterans, not most. As you do not quickly accept the labeling from others, also do not rush to label yourself.

At Your Own Pace

When reflecting, it is essential that you avoid moving too fast. Stop if an event becomes emotionally uncomfortable. The discomfort may have many expressions such as anger, anxiety, uncontrollable sadness, and fear. Continuing to reflect and dig deeper into a specific area that is surrounded by discomfort may counter progress. Therefore it is best that you take your time, and push forward while avoiding setbacks. The quest to organize and analyze past events, behavior, and thoughts for self-improvement is not a weekend task. Be patient with your effort and remember the importance of consistency. Listen to your intuition, it will say when to go forward or step back. Intuition is strengthened through the practice of meditation.

Objective Reflection

When reflecting on past events, attempt earnestly to remove any emotion attached to it. See the events objectively; as if it were the life of a stranger. It is out of control emotions causing anxiety, depression, and fear. It is out of control emotions creating adjustment barriers for veterans. As you see yourself being overtaken by emotion, make the conscious decision to let it go. Self-determination is stronger than any emotion that could ever arise. Simply ignoring emotions is the best tool for seeing events objectively. In the meditation chapter, it was highlighted that a thought without attention will fade away. The same is true here. See the emotion that seemed automatically attached to an event and then ignore it. Simple.

Forgiving

As you reflect on past events, forgive yourself for any actions, inactions, words, and thoughts. For war veterans especially, we must forgive ourselves and remove any sympathy for others; both self-condemnation and sympathy are counterproductive to adjustment.

Many condemn themselves for years over past occurrences. Many challenge the correctness of either their action or inaction. They question each event with attached emotions. These events, in the precise manner the veteran remembers, usually only live in the history book of that veteran's mind. Oftentimes, others associated with that event remember it differently or fail to remember it at all. It is a humbling experience when talking with former combat platoon members and each person recalls a single event differently. Where you remember shots fired in the area, another may remember the bullets danger close, while a third veteran has no clue what the two of you are talking about.

Seeing an event unemotionally tends to lead to forgiveness. This step, along with removing sympathy, reduces pity, anxiety, and the burden of perceived wrong. Sympathy for anyone, including yourself, begins again the cycle of emotions. The circumstance behind the sympathy is irrelevant. Remember, during reflection you view each event objectively and you see each occurrence without self-condemnation, pity, anger, hate, joy, or sympathy.

STORY – Objective Reflection Removing Automatic Emotions

While reflecting, a combat veteran remembered his first ambush. The attack was shockingly unexpected and random. He remembered the sticky heat of the Iraqi noonday and the cars speeding pass on an adjacent road. He thought of the smiling children, the waving men, and the cloaked women all seemingly welcoming of the troops. And he also remembered the Soviet machine gun delivering fire from a building, hundreds of meters away from the platoon's position. The bullets ripped the open air from across the speeding road. The smiling children, waving men, and cloaked women all vanished into an alley at once. The shooter had the high ground and there seemed little the exposed platoon could do to combat their exposure. It was a situation, as so many are in combat, of flight *then* fight.

As the shots snapped through the air, the veteran saw the wounded and the mayhem. The bloody bodies would leave impressions on all who witnessed it. The bullets, some finding their mark while others skipped off of the concrete roads, continued for minutes.

As the veteran revisited this event, he removed the emotion attached to each scene of the story. The emotions of fear and surprise as the ambush began, the charging adrenaline and excitement of battle, and the sympathy of wounded friends were all removed. These emotions had been here, attached to this story, for years. And what did those emotions bring? They brought condemnation directed at the platoon leader for exposing the platoon in such an amateurish manner. It also brought regret that return fire was not possible as it became necessary to take the wounded to the base hospital. All of that, the condemnation and the self-regret, fell away as the emotions were removed from the incident. The power struggle was reversed, and instead of an event having power the veteran took control through reflection and meditation.

Before reflection, a story was simply a story. Yet with reflection and meditation, a story is broken and the power is taken from it. The power from a story's emotion may cause continual discomfort unless it is addressed. For this veteran, instead of a first account of battle, he saw the event as a distant historical fact similar to reading a text book on a foreign war, which does not require emotions.

STORY end

Events Lose Power without Emotion

With time, unemotional reflection will cause past events to lose their power. The power of thought is a major component while reflecting. Each event is purely what you perceive it to be. What is deemed decent and permissible by some may be considered unethical by others. In addition, many will consider the event as neutral. The neutral approach allows past events to develop without the hindrance of a box.

Withdraw attention from a thought if it begins to move out of control and recur frequently. By not giving attention to a thought, it will eventually subside and pass away.

Summary

The central purpose of reflection is removing automatic emotions attached to an event. Events can vary in type and perceived importance. Some will be military based and others may be from your childhood. Each event has the potential to contribute or detract from your adjustment process.

Events tied to military service, and most others, are usually surrounded by emotions. These emotions have lingered there; attached to the event. Reflection allows an individual to remove the emotions tied to an event; emotions that cause barriers for the adjustment process. It is important to see the event objectively and without emotion to reduce the power of the event.

4
Journal

Thoughts And Behavior Are Comparative Tools Used For Journaling

'In essence, if we want to direct our lives, we must take control of our consistent actions. It's not what we do once in a while that shapes our lives, but what we do consistently'

– Tony Robbins

Journal for Improvement

Journaling is an often overlooked step for veterans adjusting to the general population. Many do not weigh the benefits of keeping a journal as opposed to judging your gains with mental memory. However, it is the best tool for chronicling where you were and where you are. Your improvements will be most noticeable here; in the journal. Areas that have worsened will also be highlighted with this important hobby.

Tracking Progress

Journaling allows a person to look at their journey. As you begin to improve and adjust into society and clear away your issues, it is easy to overlook your successes. Your successes will usually be gradual over a set of time. This gradual improvement may seem insignificant when you are going, and growing, through it. But it is there, and journaling highlights the path that you walk. For a veteran adjusting to the general population, this simple step proves valuable in tracking progress.

Journal as often as possible and give accurate and unbiased accounts of your daily life. Unbiased reporting is difficult as the reporter is not a machine. Perceptions line many reports and journal entries. Neutrality, which is strengthened in reflection, makes the difference in journaling. The journal should be an objective historical display. It should be true and naked. It is what it is. Do not make the story to be what you would like it to be. No sugar coating. Keep the story honest; raw and naked. It is what it is.

Journal Thoughts with or without Action and Action with or without Thoughts

Journal the behaviors and thoughts, or lack of thoughts, surrounding your action. These thoughts are usually seen before, during, and after an event. The thoughts associated with a behavior can be embarrassing even to you. This is why we begin explaining the behavior instead of leaving it raw. Example: Today I fought two guys at a local bar. That is raw and accurate; leave it.

Also, record the thoughts that you have not accompanied with action. Journaling can become either crowded with seemingly meaningless banter and it can also become bare with rare journals occurring only when shocking behavior takes place. Thoughts are necessary and appropriate for journal entries. An example could be 'Today, the thought of violence and anger rose repeatedly. However, I did not act on anything that I believe provoked me. I did not react when my boss chastised me in front of coworkers or when I was given additional work. Today the thought of violence and anger came yet I ignored it.' If a choice must be made, it is better to lean toward lengthiness and regularity in entries as opposed to brevity.

Some veterans experience a blank mind when committing certain acts. Some will say 'I just blacked out! I don't remember what I was thinking.' This is okay, journal your behavior without the thoughts to go along with it. If you blacked out and forgot the entire event, journal in hindsight. If there is a pattern of reckless behavior behind blanking out with anger, visit a physician.

Both thoughts and behavior are comparative tools used in journaling.

Subtle Strides

Periodically look back to appreciate your growth; you may be surprised at the strides that you have made. As said above, throughout a veteran's adjustment into the general population, the advancements will normally be subtle. It is these small and subtle changes that create the difference. If you have experienced anger, it may be difficult to notice gradual improvements. Yet, while reflecting over the past months with your journal, you may be surprised to notice less incidences of anger.

STORY – Measuring Wall

Some of us remember our parents marking the wall every couple of months when we were young and growing. We would remind our parents when we thought it was time and sometimes our parents, noticing significant grow, would summon us to the wall to get measured.

We stood with our backs to that wall - same spot every time - excited to be measured. Standing tall, our backs would be erect and our necks outstretched. The brightest smiles were on our faces as we guessed how much we grew since our last measurement.

Our parents measured us when we were young to chronicle our growth in height. As children, we never knew how much we grew until we looked back. After the measuring was completed, we would turn to face the wall. With amazement, we saw the visual difference in height that was hard to notice each day. Staring at that wall, we saw our growth in gradual stages.

For this writer, entries into a journal became a regular component in the adjustment process. I saw the emotions, the actions, and the thoughts. I saw where I came from and then I realistically challenged my improvements. I challenged my improvements by expecting more from myself in trouble areas. Areas that needed more attention I focused on specifically in meditation and reflection. Journaling helped me to see all of the areas of my adjustment process in the most objective way.

STORY end

Journal is a Correcting Tool

The journal is similar to our childhood 'measurement wall'. In both instances, it is easy to overlook progress. The child will usually believe that they either grew less or more than they actually did. It is the wall that corrects their previous beliefs and notions. The wall is the objective facts in a world filled with opinions. The same is true with the journal. Many veterans believe that they either did not grow or that they improved in areas that they did not. And just like the wall, the journal corrects our beliefs.

Much easier is it to think 'I didn't grow' or 'I still get angry'. Yet, as the veteran looks back through their journal, it may show less outbursts compared to the previous week or month. In this way, the journal is an even greater tool than the measuring wall because it directs you towards the areas in need of improvement. The journal is comprehensive. In the case of gradual improvement, one is due for celebration and not self-flogging.

Communication

A journal is also useful as a communication tool. Post Traumatic Stress Disorder and the adjustment from military to the general population may strain otherwise healthy relationships. Here, the divisive factor may seem to be the veteran's behavior when it probably is the lack of honest and open communication.

Rebuilding Old Bridges

This distancing of established relationships is more prevalent among combat veterans and their family and friends. As a veteran begins to adjust in his own way, some family and friends will back away from him. This could be due to any number of reasons associated with the veteran's behavior. The sharp edges that the veteran displays will make some feel uncomfortable. Of that group, many will be supportive and understanding of your growing process and yet others will delete your cell phone number and conveniently forget your address.

The journal works well with both of these groups. As people build support for you, you may decide to show them your journal so that they can understand the 'whys' behind your behavior. Also, the group that has distanced itself from you will understand your journey and your improvements. Relationships can be saved with this gesture. If the notion that gifts have many forms, then the gift of sharing a journal can be a priceless and memorable one for the recipient.

Sharing your journal can act as a third party by rebuilding bridges of trust and restoring comfort levels with loved ones who simply do not understand. It can also strengthen existing relationships. As a communication tool, the journal not only benefits you but all those around you. These loved ones will see your growth and they will see your effort. The first step is having the courage to share. The result of this sharing may be amazing.

STORY – Journal Used to Communicate Journey

A veteran became distant with his longtime girlfriend upon his return from combat. Previously he was a calm and level headed young man. Through his deployment, he became accustomed to a new and more predictable life. He knew when to eat, when to go on patrol, and to whom he answered. This strict control system became more relaxed as he returned from battle and entered garrison.

In garrison, he experienced a culture shock that altered his behavior and affected his entire life. He, and other loved ones in his life, noticed his lack of control over his anger; it boiled over for the most trivial reasons. In addition, he remembers becoming severely paranoid and recalls that his anxiety suppressed the quality of his life. His girlfriend saw him as a different person: a violent, hot tempered look alike of her once great boyfriend. In part, she was right. He was different. His experiences, like everyone, shaped who he became. She decided to end the relationship to maintain her own sanity. The two separated peacefully.

She failed to understand him outside of the shallow perception that he is simply different. She thought she gave him a chance to revert back into his old self. It is as if she believed that he could simply snap his fingers and move back in time. This belief of hers was unfair. A combat veteran returning from war needs to an allotment of more than a few weeks to come back to normalcy. The process of adjustment for a veteran can take a varying amount of time depending on each veteran, his willingness to improve, and the severity of his condition. For some, it is a process that needs years not weeks.

Once his girlfriend left, the soldier began looking serious into his adjustment. He started journaling. He posted journal entries regularly – each day – and focused his energies on target areas that were most in need. After a couple of months, this veteran decided to share his journal with his former girlfriend. The biggest hurdle was letting a person read his intimate thoughts. Even sharing his journal with a former girlfriend took strength and courage for him. He invited her to lunch and let her read his journal. As she looked over the pages reading each word intently, a sense of vulnerability and freedom surged his body. He was open; naked. Everything he thought and all of his actions over the past months were no longer private. He awaited her response and found her empathetic. They listened to each other and each of them learned more about the other. She forgave him since she understood the circumstances.

As of the publishing of this book, the two have remained friends.

STORY end

Trust and Comfort

Naturally, many veterans are uncomfortable sharing their journal. In such cases these veterans should understand that trust speaks volumes. There are trustworthy people around all of us. If they have distanced themselves from you in your adjustment period, the journal may become the best bridge to mend the relationship. Once you open up and explain things in truth, the relationship may be stronger than ever before. Remember, trust is the key.

Summary

The journal allows us to gauge our progress and determine if we are moving ahead or taking steps backward. The journal will also allow us to objectively perceive how we are advancing in problematic areas. More than just a tool for chronicling gains, the journal can be used as a communication device. Permitting friends and family to read your journal may take some bravery but it may also prove beneficial. The result may be either the mending of a former relationship or the strengthening of an existing one.

5
Exercise and Eat Healthy

Eat And Exercise Like Your Life Depends On It

'If man made it don't eat it'

– Jack Lalanne

'Exercising without eating the proper foods is like plowing a field and not putting any seed into the ground. Nothing would grow out of it'

–Arnold Schwarzenegger

Your Body Deserves It

Eating and exercise not only affects your physical wellness but also your mental capacities. You should eat and exercise like your life depends on it. Our body and mind are important enough for us to devout time and energy into protecting them. Poor eating habits can detract from the previous chapters. Meditation and reflection are more difficult when your body is falling apart and full of junk.

While adjusting to the general population, it is normal for many to overlook this important part of the process. They will focus on their thoughts and behavior and rightfully so; these are important areas. However, it is exercise and eating habits that influence our thoughts and behaviors.

Conscious of our Eating

Be conscious of what, why, and how much you are eating. Anxiety, stress, and depression can affect all three of these categories. Each of these factors can keep a person camping out in the kitchen or snacking around the clock. These comfort foods are used to cope with a number of issues. Depression and anxiety attached to service is one such issue. Here, the veteran must take it from the top and begin to meditate and reflect. However, it comes down to denying yourself of these comfort foods and understanding that they are potentially reducing the quality of your life in various ways.

Comfort Foods

Some veterans have designated comfort foods, which usually make them uncomfortable with how they look later in the week. These foods are usually sugary and provide an instant get-away from perceived issues. This leads into the 'why' of eating. Catching the impulse prior to acting is important in challenging yourself. Food, like many things, can become very addictive if not corrected. It is best to attack the addiction before it starts. This is not always a possibility, so bring your addiction into meditation to see it objectively. How much you are eating moves parallel with addiction. Ask yourself why then meditate for improvement.

Another component of this book's plan, journaling, is also a great way to improve diet choices. Freely journal your meal and snack selection. It could be helpful to connect food choices with daily events and emotions.

Balanced Diet is Somewhere in the Middle

So the answer is a balanced diet. This cliché, said over and over with variation is a foundation for life. There are many talking heads and personal trainers barking the same order. Others have written books and magazine articles not only on what to eat healthy but when to eat. Each has their own approach and it is best that you follow something that works. Try to stay somewhere in the middle of the many extremes that will be present in this field.

There are books and columns on a number of eating dogmas: eat only meat, eat on fruit, eat as if you lived 10,000 years ago, sleep more so you will not have time to eat, and so many more. As said, study the basics of nutrition and try to avoid the extreme fringes.

Fat Day

However, give yourself a day every week or month to eat without restrictions; to be undisciplined. This means that once a week you pull out the pint of double chunky chocolate chip ice cream and have at it! If you decide to have an undisciplined day each week, you will notice that the disciplined part of your week will become less of a chore with time. After a while, you will stop anticipating this 'Fat Day' and even stop going over the top as you had before. Instead of going through a pint of your favorite ice cream, you may decide to just have a couple large cookies after dinner. As time goes on, it may be less than this and the treats will be spread out over a period of time longer than a week. Eventually, your fat day will move from a week to monthly or, perhaps, quarterly.

Alcoholism

Another common practice among veterans is trying to find answers in a bottle. Veterans turn to alcohol for as many reasons as there are alcoholic veterans. Although there are many reasons, the denominator remains the same: you are solving nothing. Similar to over-eating, or eating poorly to capture an instant escape, alcohol provides a temporary cloak to an ugly wound. As stated in the first chapter, avoidance of the problem will likely solve nothing and will usually cause the issue to worsen.

STORY – Alcohol is a Poor Coping Tool

Upon leaving the US Army, Patrick developed the basic growing pains associated with a veteran's adjustment. Chiefly, he experienced and battled anxiety and depression. So many options and issues seemed to come at him too quickly. Patrick did not feel that the military's process for outgoing soldiers was enough to prepare him for the real world. *What direction do I go in? Should I enroll in school, get a job, or both? What is next for me?* These questions were not unique to Patrick; many veterans ask themselves the same questions directly after leaving the service.

As a coping tool for the uncertainty of life and his inability to secure a job, Patrick began to drink more than usual. Extra beer here and a double shot there. It escalated to a point that he began drinking a couple glasses of wine each morning to get his day going. This sounds bizarre to some and familiar to others, but for Patrick this allowed him to ignore – not remove – the pressing issues.

The issue was that he was suffering from poor adjustment into the general population for a number of reasons. One of those reasons was his failure to successfully prepare prior to leaving the military. Another reason was that he underestimated the cultural difference or believed it would be a simple hurdle. The culture shock from the military should be expected to some degree. Therefore, all troops should prepare for it.

The wine in the morning kept Patrick stable until he drunk more wine and liquor at night. It was an ongoing cycle. This persisted for a couple of months until he finally realized the harm of his behavior. We simply cannot use liquor, or any other drug, to suppress issues. After understanding that his issues needed to be addressed and corrected, Patrick began to implement the plan in this book.

The drinking did not stop all at once. He reduced his intake over the course of a few weeks. Exercise and journal entries helped him overcome the bane of alcoholism. Meditation and reflection allowed Patrick to address issues that were ripping his life to pieces.

From this period of sobriety onwards, Patrick has not taken a drink of alcohol. He rehabilitated his life by first taking responsibility for what was happening in it. A major constituent part of his recovery was his comprehending that there are absolutely no solutions to current issues in extreme alcohol consumption; there are only more negative issues waiting to attach themselves to Patrick and his family.

STORY end

Put it On Track

Still not sure of the best way to put your diet on track? First, avoid fast food as a staple of your diet. Sure, most fast food chains have a few healthy options now and it is the easy and convenient way, but begin to make an effort toward cooking healthy meals and packing lunches.

Get your Apron

Packing lunches may prove not only the healthier choice but also the cheapest. Packed lunches are even cheaper than the fast food joint that you past everyday on your way to work. This do-it-yourself plan is explorative and fun. If you enjoy cooking you are ahead of the crowd. If you are kitchen illiterate, the learning process does not have to be a trial and error snooze fest. Make cooking fun by studying recipes online and buying or renting cookbooks from your local library. There is a large section on cooking recipes and many will spark your interest. Everyone likes to eat (at least everyone I know) so you are bound to see some style that you like. In addition, cooking classes are a great way to meet new and interesting people. Classes are available in markets and small groups.

You may already have a particular cultural cuisine in mind, or you may find something that you never would have expected yourself to enjoy. Italian, Mexican, and Chinese are two of the more popular choices. Some of the more difficult dishes would be Ethiopian and Thai. Whatever you choose, have fun in the kitchen and use this time to invite friends and family over to help prepare and experiment the meals. Not only is cooking a great social tool, it is also another one of the hidden therapies that reduces anxiety.

Exercising for Life

Exercise has more value than keeping you aesthetically pleasing. It also performs wonders for your mind. We have heard of the runner's high, which seems to be an urban legend to many, but there are also benefits to exercise when the physical exertion stops.

Mind Power

Exercise improves our ability to cope with the anxiety, stress, and depression affecting many veterans. In addition to building a healthier mind, exercise also makes us smarter. Your ability to weigh the consequences of your actions and dive into your thoughts will improve greatly once you maintain a consistent exercise regime. In addition, your time in meditation and reflection will become more effective once exercise becomes a staple in your life.

Attitude Shift

Coupled with healthy food choices, consistent exercise may have the most notable effect on your life. It too is usually the part of your regime that others notice the soonest. Before the standard compliments of 'Man you look trim,' many others will notice your change in attitude and behavior.

A veteran's attitude towards his life is more ambitious as he embarks on the healthier path. Exercise is a vent for tension and anxiety. If any veteran is oblivious to their own improvement, others around him will notice his breakthroughs. Many of your friends, family, and coworkers have caught on to your adjustment journey. They have noticed the anxiety, or the paranoia, or the temper, or the depression. As a support cast, most choose not to address this directly; however, as you improve they will be quick to congratulate.

Your Workout Regimen To Get Back On Track

As a personal trainer and exercise enthusiast, I present the following workout schedule as a beginner and intermediate plan. As I am sure you are aware of, you should consult with your primary care physician before undertaking anything strenuous; which includes this plan. You may also find it necessary to give this plan to your existing trainer if you have one. He or she may look at this and form new ideas or create a new workout plan with this regime part of it.

Seven Days

This plan is built on seven days. Within these seven days are five workout days and two rest days. As you will soon notice, the workouts segment areas of the body. Segmentation is simply focusing the workout on a few muscle groups in a select area. This allows for a better recovery than the generic full body workout. A segmented workout plan also allows for short intense workouts. Spending hour after hour in a gym causes boredom; which leads to frustration, which leads to quitting. To avoid the boredom, frustration, and quitting this workout plan is designed for high intensity sessions that do not exceed an hour.

Listen to Your Body

Before you begin any workout, remember that your body is boss. If it says enough, call it a day. There is no reason pushing yourself to your limit at this stage. It is also worthy of note that a single loss day at the gym will not diminish your conditioning. Most trainers agree that you have to be inactive for about two weeks before your conditioning level begin to decrease. Anything before that is all in your head.

Day 1

This plan can be either the first day of the week, Sunday, or the first day of the business week, Monday. Or it can be whatever day inside the week that you read this book and get fired up. The point is to keep the start date close; none of that 'I'll start on the first of the month' or 'I'll get at it in the New Year'. Get to it as soon as possible. This is part of your recovery and the hardest move is the first step.

Morning – Cardio

No longer than 60 minutes. This will vary for obvious reasons. People have lesser or greater ability than others is one reason. Prior and existing injuries are another hindrance to cardiovascular exercise. As a former Infantry Reconnaissance Scout, I enjoy the long run, but others find running unforgiving on their lower joints. These individuals will usually prefer swimming or biking over running. Whichever exercise is chosen, try to build yourself to 60 minutes.

60 minutes is not a magic number randomly drawn out of a top hat. This is the average time that blood sugar levels drop during intense workout. This can cause a host of other factors to play a role

in your workout. To keep it simple, shoot for 60 intense minutes. Age and conditioning level of the athlete and the intensity of the workout are variables that will alter the standard 60 minute rule. However, it is best to stick with this rule for beginner and intermediate training.

As a note to walkers, try to walk four miles in the hour. This 15 minute per mile pace should be your goal if not your standard.

Evening – This workout will focus on chest and triceps

Eat a couple of hours before this strength workout. Begin doing a pyramid of pushups from your maximum effort down one for 10 sets. Sounds confusing? Not really. As an example, one person may max his pushup at 50. Therefore, his sets of 10 would have repetitions of 50, 49, 48, 47, 46, 45, 44, 43, 42, and 41 for a grand total of 455 pushups. Once this pyramid is complete, stretch your chest and prepare for your triceps workout.

Stretch your chest by clasping your hands behind your back and lifting your chest while extending your arms. Another chest stretch is to place your hand on a wall and gently turn your torso away from the wall. Hold both of these stretches for 3-5 seconds.

A couple of dumbbells lying around the house never hurt anyone and would prove very useful for home workouts. If you do not have a dumbbell, pick up a gallon of milk or water or anything else that can be managed easily with a single hand. The next exercise is the triceps extensions.

At a standing position, take the dumbbell with one hand and lift it overhead. Your arm should be straight in this starting position. From here, bend the elbow 90 degrees and lift back to the starting position. Perform your maximum then complete three sets of your maximum minus three repetitions. For example, your maximum may be 15. This is one set. Your next three sets would then be 12 each, for a total workout of 15, 12, 12, and 12.

Stretch your triceps after this workout. You can stretch your triceps by straightening your arm above your head. Bend the elbow and attempt to place your hand in the center of your back while avoiding discomfort. Place your other hand on your bent elbow and apply slight pressure downwards. Hold the stretch for 3-5 seconds per arm.

Hydration and Weight Loss

Remember to drink water freely throughout all workouts. Some trainers tell you to not drink water and after the workout they weigh you. Keep in mind that the majority of the weight you think you lost is only water-weight; it does not count as you will gain it back as soon as you rehydrate. The weight you want to lose is fat, and this is done incrementally. A good rate of weight loss is 2-4 pounds a week, anything more than this is probably caused by malnutrition or a lack of water-weight.

Day 2

After the two workouts yesterday, you will either be exhausted or excited. Regardless, we are going to relax on cardiovascular exercise in the morning and complete a strength workout in the afternoon or night. As this workout schedule is segmented, you will find that as you are sore in one area, the area that you are currently working on will be fresh. Ah, the beauty of segmentation! Sometimes you will feel a whole body fatigue or soreness and choose to rest until you feel comfortable to begin again. But do not allow yourself to take too long of a break. A one day breather is plenty.

Afternoon or Evening – Today we are focusing on back and biceps

A couple of hours after your last meal find a pull-up bar apparatus. If the pull-up bar is outside, take your dumbbells or dumbbell alternatives with you. Today we will perform a full pyramid using both the overhand grip and the underhand grip. For many, the overhand grip, the pull-up, is more difficult than the underhand grip, the chin-up. So we will begin with the most difficult option while our energy is still fresh.

Jump on the bar with hands at shoulder length. Perform your maximum amount of pull-ups then perform a set with one repetition less than your maximum. Continue for a total of 4 sets. For example, if your maximum repetition of pull-ups is 10, the remaining sets would be 9, 8, and 7. At this point, take a stretch break. Get those muscles ready for the climb back up the pyramid. This time, however, we are performing chin-ups.

Grab the bar at shoulder length and complete the pyramid by going from the last set of repetitions back to your original maximum. For example, in this scenario you would start at 7 followed by sets of 8, 9, and 10 repetitions. Your muscles are burning and your mind may be telling you to quit, but focus on the goal and take the rests that you feel you need. Try to keep all of the rests less than 30 seconds.

After the pull-ups and chin-ups are completed, get another good stretch for your back. Stretch your back muscles by standing erect with feet shoulder width apart and placing your left hand on your left hip while the right arm is straight above your head. Move your torso in the direction of your left hip. Move slowly to avoid injury. Once you reach your limit of flexibility, hold for 3-5 seconds. Complete on the right side.

Now comes the second part of the workout: bicep curls. If you have two dumbbells equal in weight this workout will be quicker. If you only have one then the rests between sets will be shorter. As one arm rests, the other can begin its repetitions.

Perform your maximum of bicep curls. This is followed by three sets of your maximum minus three repetitions. For example, if your maximum was 22 repetitions; the following three sets will consist of 19 repetitions. The total breakdown would then be 22, 19, 19, and 19.

Last piece of this workout is the bicep stretch. The bicep stretch is similar to the wall chest stretch. If you are outside, grab a vertical pole with a single hand and stretch your bicep by turning your body away from the pole. The arm must be fully extended to maximize the benefit of this stretch. Hold each stretch for 3-5 seconds and repeat on the opposite arm.

Day 3

You are doing great at this point; so great that you have earned a scheduled day off. Go about your day in a typical manner; just avoid strenuous exercise when possible.

Fat Day

Reminder: do you remember 'fat day'? It is the day that we relax our dietary standards every so often, be it once a week or month. Well, this rest day is not the best for fat day. Choose a day with at least one scheduled workout to pig out. The fat day is best when coupled with a day that you are burning the most calories. It seems natural for many to reach for the pint of ice cream on a day when they are not exercising. Yet the best day for increased calories is the day when more calories are exerted through exercise. Keep this in mind.

Also, at the onset of a responsible diet plan you may countdown from fat day to fat day. This will be your little holiday as you undertake a healthier diet. Eventually however, the memories of the triple chunky chocolate ice cream with the fudge brownie will fade away. Over a period, the fat day will not include fanfare; it will simply be a day that sneaks up on you and that you may choose to ignore and bypass.

Day 4

Now you are well rested and energetic for another workout. You may still experience some soreness from day 2, but generally the pain is insignificant. However, listen to your body and the signs it gives. Know and discern between the sign of soreness and the sign of injury. Usually they are quite easy to differentiate. If any soreness persists, or you are unsure whether it a simple muscle soreness or injury, seek guidance from your primary care physician.

Sharpen Your Determination

In addition, discern not only between muscle soreness and injury, but also between these two and a lack of interest. Lack of interest, or boredom, is common within the first few weeks of exercise; especially for beginners. As the initial fire subsides, it is the determination that must remain. Determination is sometimes passed on externally through trainers and coaches, but the best determination comes from within. You need to understand your goal of working out. Goals feed determination and determination is the keystone when beginning a new workout plan.

Many times it is challenging to push through the soreness and keep the determination strong. The earlier stages after adopting a consistent workout regime normally are the toughest. This stage takes the body and mind from their norm. Past this stage and fitness becomes part of your life. It will enter the cultural norms of who you are and what you do. This persistent determination is not only the key to a successful workout plan but it is also the key factor when eating healthy. As you change your diet, the first few weeks are characterized by cravings for sugar. These cravings will eventually lessen and decline.

Morning – Here we go; back to cardio

We are building ourselves to 60 minutes of tough, strenuous cardio. Therefore, if our current ability is a 20 minute jog, we consider it as a successful building block. The next week we will look for a 25 minute jog at the same pace. The same may be expected for the following week. This is not a magic trick; the best way to extend your run performance is through speed training and determination.

The speed training may take the form of intervals or sprints. Both work well. With intervals, design a 20 minute jog and choose a faster pace for a designated span within this jog. There may be three, two-minute running intervals that increase your heart rate significantly. This will develop a stronger ability to extend your run time at the original pace; thus bringing your jog time from 20 to 25 minutes and so forth.

For sprints, remember to warm up before the run. It is a preferred technique of many runners to use the first five minutes of a run as a warm up for loosening muscles. After the warm up, a faster past is taken for the remainder of the run. Stretching, in this method of running, is performed at the end of the jog. Others choose to stretch before running, but it is important to remember that stretching without a warm up can potentially be harmful. For the sprint, the approach is to warm up with a soft jog, stretch, then enter into your sprinting routine. After the sprints are completed, have a cool down jog, and stretch once more. A good and reasonable time for both the warm up and cool down jogs is five minutes.

Be Smart

Bear in mind that the morning cardio should be strenuous but not extreme in the beginning stages. A one hour run in a southern Californian desert is an irresponsible exercise choice for a beginner. Sometimes we allow our excitement to transform into foolishness. Consistency is the key. Exercise should become a habitual enjoyment and not simply a means to an end. And this way – smart consistency – a veteran can build herself to that desert run.

Evening – For the evening workout, we will focus on legs and the lower back

Before we go into this workout, remember to not hesitate in adding to this workout schedule. Any favorite exercises that are not included should be added to increase the workout experience. Nothing here is rigid. As a suggestion, follow the segmentation scheme to allow for better targeting and recovery of key muscle groups. Likewise, favorite stretches that are not included in this workout plan should be added at the veteran's discretion.

The first exercise is the squat. We will perform two variations for a total of six sets. When completing squats, as in all exercises, it is important to be aware of your body and form. When squatting, move your pelvis back into a sitting position until your leg forms a 90 degree angle. At this position, your knees should NOT be ahead of your toes. If you look down at this position and you cannot see your toes or shoe top caps then you are probably performing the squat incorrectly. Through the squat exercise, keep your hands behind your head with fingers interlocked.

For variation 1, the starting position is a wide squat stance. A wide stance is approximately one foot larger than shoulder width distance. The feet should point away from the body slightly. This variation focuses on the inner thigh. Perform your maximum amount of repetitions then complete two sets of your maximum minus three repetitions. For example, if your maximum repetitions are 40 squats then the next two sets will be 37 repetitions each. Your sets will be 40, 37, and 37.

With variation 2, the starting position is a narrow squat stance. This position separates the feet at a distance of 4-6 inches. The toes all point forward. The quadriceps is the primary focus of the narrow squat stance. After you stretch from the previous squats, perform your maximum amount of repetitions followed by two sets of your maximum repetitions minus three. For example, your sets may appear as 25, 22, and 22.

After the squat exercise, stretch the quadriceps and groin with the following stretches. The quadriceps stretch is completed by bending your knee and holding your ankle close to your body while standing. Hold this stretch for 3-5 seconds. It may be necessary to place a hand on a wall or something stationary for balance.

Complete the butterfly stretch for the groin muscles. While sitting on the floor, bring the soles of your feet together. Grab your ankles and push your thighs down with your elbows. Complete two sets of 5 seconds.

The next exercise is the calf raise. Toes are pointed forward and feet are shoulder width apart. Lift your heels as far as possible while avoiding discomfort. Lower your heels without letting them touch the floor. For balance reasons, you may find it necessary to touch a wall or hold a chair. If this exercise proves too easy, perform single leg calf raises instead. Complete a set of your maximum repetitions followed by three sets of your maximum repetitions minus three. For example, your sets may appear as 19, 16, 16, and 16.

Stretch the calf muscles by placing both hands on a wall and slightly bending the left leg while extending the right leg. The extended leg is stretched by placing the heel firmly on the ground. Hold the stretch for 3-5 seconds and repeat on the opposite leg. Throughout this stretch the back must remain erect.

The last exercise of the day is the low back extension. This exercise begins in the prone position. With feet together and fingers interlocked behind the head, lift your torso as high as possible while avoiding discomfort. Perform your maximum set of repetitions followed by two sets of your maximum repetitions minus three. Your effort may be summarized as 12, 9, and 9.

Stretch the low back muscle group by moving to the supine position. Bring your knees to your chest and grasp your hands across your knees. Push down slightly and hold the stretch for 3-5 seconds.

Day 5

There will be no morning cardiovascular workout for today. We are allowing a rest in anticipation of a tough and intense Day 6.

Evening – Today we are focusing on abdominals

There are four exercises in this workout. Add more as you become more comfortable in this area. In addition, you may also decide to add abdominal exercises throughout the seven day workout plan. For many, abdominal exercises do not cause severe soreness. However, it is best to allow at least one day of rest between each abdominal workout in your seven day regime.

The first exercise is the basic crunch. Lie on your back, supine position, and plant the soles of your feet on the floor. At this position, your knees should point to the ceiling. Forearms should be crossed, and rested, on your chest. Lift your shoulder blades a few inches off the ground then return to the starting position. Perform 200 repetitions at your own pace while taking as many rests as needed. This can take either a few minutes or more than 10 minutes depending on your fitness level.

The next exercise is the supine bicycle. Lying on your back, your thighs should create a perpendicular angle with the floor and your knees should be bent at a 90 degree angle. Fingers are interlocked behind the neck yet they do not pull the head or neck. The first move is to bring the right elbow to the left knee and the left knee towards the right elbow. Return to the starting position then complete the next repetition by bringing the left elbow and right knee together. The goal is for the elbow and the knee to touch. If they do not touch, crunch as far as you can without discomfort. One set is a repetition to both sides. Complete 100 sets taking rests as needed. Remember to keep your form intact. As the sets and repetitions pile on, it is better to take a break and perform the exercise properly then to rush through the workout in a sloppy, wasteful fashion.

The third exercise is the supine leg lift. Lie on your back with arms to your side and feet together. Lift your legs in unison into a perpendicular position with the floor. Lower your legs to the floor in a controlled manner to complete the repetition. As you become tired during this workout, be careful not to simply throw the legs to the ground on the descent. The heart of the exercise is in the resistance during the descent into the starting position. Be mindful of form. Throughout this movement, the upper body remains stationary. Perform 50 repetitions taking breaks as needed.

The last exercise in this abdominal workout is the plank. The plank builds core stability and strength. It is performed by bringing your body into a modified pushup position. The body is brought to a lifted prone position with the toes and forearms as the points of contact with the ground or mat. The toes and forearms are both shoulder width apart. Using a timing device, either a stopwatch or the second hand on a clock, time the following exercise sets. Perform 4 sets of 30 seconds each. Take a 30 second break in between sets. Gradually challenge yourself during the plank exercise. Instead of 30 seconds, next week attempt one minute.

Prone abdominal stretch is performed by lying in the prone position and pushing your torso erect. While performing this stretch, keep the pelvis planted on the floor and the arms straight. Bring the head back and focus the eyes on the ceiling. Perform this stretch twice holding each stretch for a count of 3-5 seconds.

Day 6

Today is a day of intense cardio work. This morning's cardio will be the only workout of the day. The goal is to push yourself while keeping the session inside of the 60 minute limit. That limit is still there for the same reasons. However, if you want to venture past this barrier, be sure to bring along a sports drink or sports bar to enhance your workout and keep your body performing at a high level. Yet for most, the workout can still be compacted into 60 intense minutes; especially in the beginning and intermediate stages.

Creativity

This is also a great time to try something new; if you have biked on days 1 and 4, swim in the pool for an hour. It is also a great time to increase the duration of your previous workouts: if you have run 30 minutes on days 1 and 4, run 60 minutes at a slower pace. Be creative. There are many possibilities to add change into your workout plan. A good hike with a large pack is also a good choice. Hiking up a mountain with friends will be plenty of fun.

As a guideline for runners, it is a general rule of thumb to note that an increase in intensity should not be coupled with an increase in time. It is best to not stretch your exercise duration while also performing at your maximum capacity. This day of cardiovascular focus means that the duration of the exercise(s) of choice is pushed while your own exertion remains manageable.

Another creative option is to mix cardiovascular exercises. A gym is valued here for its convenience, yet outside may prove just as good. An example plan for mixed cardio would be 30 minute swimming followed by 30 minutes jogging. This is also a great way to stay motivated as the change in exercise increases the enthusiasm in the entire plan.

A last option for creativity is to go into a boxing or mixed martial arts gym on this cardio blast day. These sports require high cardiovascular strength paired also with muscle endurance. If you are not interested in fighting, let the trainers, coaches, and gym owners know as you enter the building. Most boxing and MMA establishments have classes for learners that amount to an energy draining aerobics session. And most are tailor made for an hour of intensity. The added benefit is hitting the heavy bags and blowing off steam as your learn crosses and arm bars.

Day 7

You did it. The first week is completed and behind you. Hopefully you have tracked your progress and any aches and pains experienced along the way within your journal. Day 7 is a rest day. Use this time to alter the workout schedule in any way that fits you best. The tracking of the workouts is a great way to see what did or did not work.

Each day after you work out, jot down what you completed and the time it took. Give commentary on the effectiveness of the exercise as well. Even if you enjoyed each exercise within week one, it is still necessary to switch the exercises often. Changing the exercises allows your mind to stay attentive and your muscles to stay fully engaged.

Day 1 of the following work out week begins tomorrow. Be ready.

STORY – Marathon for Adjustment

Exercise can assist in proper adjustment to the general population. In combination with healthy eating choices, the results can be amazing.

A Marine, who served in Afghanistan, picked up weight after discharging from the military. Instead of making excuses for his weight, he made goals to target it. The goals were to eat healthy and run a marathon. He trained day after day, stretching his runs longer and longer. The weight melted off from the weeks of intense training.

Three months from the time he set the goal, he was on the starting line of the San Francisco Marathon. In the process, his anxiety and depression improved dramatically. Without exercise and healthy eating, it is safe to say that his improvements would not have been as pronounced in such a quick span of time.

STORY stop

Summary

Eating healthy and exercising regularly helps in the adjustment process. Current eating habits may be less than satisfactory, but the benefits of change are always there. In a busy life, it is easy to eat fast food and other quick choices as a means of convenience. Here, we want to keep the convenience and add a healthier option. The best option usually is cooking your meals at home and bringing them with you. Your cooking abilities may be at a level that you are comfortable with. If they are not, have fun with the educational process. Cookbooks and online tutorials and cooking groups are great ways to sharpen your cooking prowess.

Exercise benefits not only the body but also the mind. Exercising regularly has been shown to help with the adjustment process by lessening depression, anxiety, and stressful thoughts. The workout plan is based around a week schedule. At times, it may seem like a chore and even a waste of time. Self-determination is the only personal trainer during these times. Self-determination will be the difference between taking a 'short break' and pushing through to your goals; it will also be the difference between 'not feeling up to it' for the early workout and running those 4 miles even when you want to sleep for another couple of hours. In both examples, the only difference is self-determination.

Keep the workout fresh by adding exercises that will serve you best and deleting those that are too easy or uncomfortable. Stay fresh and stay fit.

6
Friends

When You Evolve, Your Crowd Has No Choice But To Evolve As Well

'If I can't change the people around me, I change the people around me'

– Chuck D

The Right Crowd

Keep your closest crowd of friends energetic, optimistic, and ambitious. Add new faces to your group of friends; new faces who are in line with who you are and not simply who you were. Surround yourself with positive goal seeking individuals. So much of the personality of our closest friends rubs off on us and us on them. We all remember our parents advising us to choose the right crowd. They also spoke about purging your crowd of 'bad apples'. Your adjustment requires a similar approach.

It Starts with you

Be calculating and critical in who you spend your valuable time with. Look for the goal oriented person with optimistic views of life and their possibilities for success. These individuals will challenge you intellectually and draw out your capabilities. Finding the right people to fill your circle is not a sizeable chore. It is neither necessary to put an ad in the local paper nor hold interviews at a local coffee house.

This is not an external quest.

Likeness Attracts

The trick to bringing the best people into your acquaintance and friendship is to improve yourself. Work on yourself first. Fix the unfavorable behaviors and thoughts that have become habitual for you; the negativity, the anxiety, the pessimism. If you do not want friends with those traits, then you must correct these within yourself. Think of it like this, if you are not depressed and sad, would you befriend someone who is? Or would you mentor them? Most would mentor this person and try to help them shake those ailments off. The individuals you meet will also be attracted to likeness. They will be more willing to help a pessimistic person before bringing them within their net of friends at a dinner party.

Meditation Improves Your Crowd

Meditation is a great tool for stripping an individual of unwanted thoughts and behaviors. As a person meditates, he begins to view his thoughts objectively. He views the areas that need improvement and acts accordingly. As unwanted traits begin detaching themselves from your personality, others with now similar personalities and traits will become attracted to you. It is the easiest way to make the type of acquaintance you desire. It is also the most efficient. You dropped paranoia in exchange for trust; now you begin attracting trustworthy people. You removed bitterness and adopted openness, now your circle can become open-minded. And the same for optimism, love, kindness, and so on. As you evolve as a person, your crowd has no choice but to evolve.

Relevant Conversations, Stay on Topic

A central element in adjusting to the general population is keeping your conversations relevant to everyone. It is easy to begin telling war stories and offensive army jokes to break a silence, but this dialogue should be saved for another time. Instead, study up and start conversations on current events, history, and the latest books. Your journey through the military and into the adjustment process is not a hot topic and it is better left for non-social conversations. Use your reflection time to draw up any stories. Address them there and leave them there. There are also veteran groups that allow a person to open up with others who are sure to understand.

Teach and Assist

Once your adjustment is complete and you have shed some individuals from your inner circle, be first in teaching others to improve. Teaching keeps the principles found in this book close to you. You may begin by teaching the friends who have left you during your process.

Once you removed your depression and your depressed friends, find them and provide them with words of encouragement.

Defensive and Confrontational

Many people are defensive and will move into a shell once you begin identifying their areas that are in need of improvement. Some will ignore you, some will attack you verbally, and others will listen. If only 1 of 7 of your past friends listens to you then you are a great success and should guide that person as much as you can. Use the pointers highlighted in this book to provide the best mentorship. Identification of an issue, meditation, reflection, exercise, healthy diet, and keeping a journal are beneficial whether someone is a veteran or not. You may find it best to provide a small class on the book. The pointers in this book will also speak to the hearts of young people raised in tough neighborhoods and those battling drug abuse. This book then can be labeled not only for veterans but also for anyone seeking self-improvement.

Summary

Our friends are a mirror of who we are. They are an accurate snapshot of our personalities. Attempting to choose the best circle of friends, which is very important, without first making an effort towards self improvement and correction is a fallacy. The best option is to work on your own traits and remove the unwanted areas from your personality. If you suffer from depression and a pessimistic view of life, it is more sufficient to work on yourself then your friendships. As you correct certain areas, your acquaintances and friends will either move with you or will be left behind. Either way, your circle of friends will spontaneously improve once you improve.

As friends become former friends and as you meet others in need, it is essential that you go back and assist them in their journey. Many times this will be met with resistance. More than likely, the person will be defensive and argumentative when you attempt to help them through their depression or anger. Some will stay angry but others will listen.

It is imperative that you mentor where you can. Being a mentor allows the tenants of this book to stay fresh and relevant in your mind. Once mentoring, you may choose to explain the principles covered in this book. It may begin as a one-on-one mentorship and may evolve into a class that meets regularly. The goal is to improve and help others improve.

7
New Experiences

Your Attitude Must Change

'Your attitude, not your aptitude, will determine your altitude'

– Zig Ziglar

'Live with passion!'

– Tony Robbins

Enjoy Life

Fake it until you make it. Yes, you read that line right. Adjustment disorders and post traumatic stress disorder may force veterans into a shell of comfort. The comfort comes in many forms, be it movies, video games, or solitude. They may seem harmless as you relax on a recliner, but they are counterproductive to your recovery.

Force if Necessary

At times you have to force yourself to enjoy life; force yourself to create new experiences. The word *force* may create an image of unwillingness and a push against the grain. Leaving your comforts may be just that at first. Yet at each stage in life you have to assert your will over yourself. Through determination you must shape your life in the image you desire.

Get Out of the House

There are many areas to touch when bringing someone out of their comfort zone and pushing them towards growth. The first and most important area is leaving the house. Do not stay indoors around the clock no matter how comfortable it seems. It does not matter if you have three game consoles, two 60 inch televisions, and a top of the line computer. It does not matter. The goal here is to leave your residence so that you can experience the beautiful world beyond your door. The colors of nature, the crisp morning air, the engaging neighborly discussions are all waiting for you. And here is where many have to force themselves out of the door.

As a veteran, you have much more to offer your community than reclusiveness. You also have more to give than grouchy similarity once you leave your home. It is often stated that your attitude is more important in life than your intelligence. A healthy attitude draws people close to you and gives you an optimistic view of life. This attitude is in your grasp. You are the creator of your reality.

CULTURE SHOCK   67

Attitude

Remember that the process of choosing friends begins with altering your thoughts and behavior. Creating new experiences works in the same manner. A grouchy person or a person living in the past has difficulty enjoying life. Your attitude must change. This implies that your thoughts must change. This quest leads us back to meditation and reflection discussed above.

As our perception of life improves so too will our attitude. Fresh air, sunlight, social contact, and a positive attitude all affect your experiences. Experiences are what you make of them. It is quite common for two people to experience a single event from two distinctly different viewpoints. Attitude and perception shape the experience for each person. Therefore, it is important to check your attitude at the door each day.

STORY – Let the Present Replace the Past

During a combat operation in Iraq, a dear friend of mine was wounded. The day began like any other: chow hall, personal hygiene, patrol prep. Yet in this mission he was knocked over with a single round delivered from the enemy. Under the hail of bullets and a pinching pain, he managed to remain alert and responsive.

From the next week onward he began excessively retelling his Purple Heart story. As his roommate, I was told the story a few dozen times; even though I was present at the firefight. He told the same story with a few variations time after time and day after day. Not showing sensitivity, many began to grow irritated at his repetitiveness. They mocked or ignored him. Yet as he told this past story, it was apparent that he was reliving it. He was there. Still there. He was still being shot at, he was continuously hit by a hidden enemy, and he freshly remembered his overwhelming pain and anger. He never left that event.

Leaving the military, this event continued to play and dominate his life. He put himself in a shell. He stayed indoors and relived his past. This was the wholeness of his reality. This veteran moved into his parents' home after a short time on his own. He was simply too concerned with the past to create new experiences. Instead of giving his attention to his passions and gifts, he focused on an event that happened years before. He was more concerned with the past than he was with the present. His adjustment would seem a failure in the eyes of most rational individuals.

Meditation and reflection is very important for veterans in this predicament. Meditation lessens reactive emotions strung to past events. Reflection allows a veteran to address a past event on his or her own terms. Those terms are in a controlled and objective manner. Controlling the event consists of stopping and starting as your comfort level allows.

Controlling the event also means that we do not think about it around the clock. We have better things to think about throughout our day. An event is viewed objectively when we do not react in an automatic manner. Reflecting on being shot should not bring depression or hate for the shooter. Just see it objectively and move on.

Journalism – always important – is a vital element in the adjustment process for veterans reliving past traumatic events. Not all veterans are as wordy when dealing with this issue. Some become introverted simply relive and rethink events without sharing with others. Journalism is a tool to express your deepest feelings in confidence. Past events that have clung onto your mind should be given a detailed description. As the veteran settles in the regime of meditation and reflection, he must be sure to track key areas of his adjustment. An automatic emotion tied to a traumatic event is one such area. The veteran will most likely notice the power of the past events diminishing well before he documents it in the journal.

STORY end

Conscious of Our Thoughts and Behaviors

Question: How can we expect improvement when we trod the same roads? It is imperative that we put forth the effort to correct our thoughts and behavior; they rarely correct themselves. Honesty and determination are essential in this quest. First we must be honest with ourselves. Am I where I want to be? Are my thoughts and behavior ideal for who I want to become? This step cannot be overlooked. Once you have identified a need for correction, you can direct your attention to that area for improvement. From there, you can move through the steps in this book.

Success at Your Own Pace

This veteran's story, given above, did not end at his parent's home. Moving at his own pace, he began to meditate and journal his thoughts, his behavior, and that firefight. He wrote in detail and focused on his goals for improvement. First it was a chore, but eventually he made enough improvements to enroll in college and move into an apartment of his own. There are no dead ends and no hopeless veteran cases! Each veteran can make a successful transition into the general population.

Volunteering

Volunteering regularly is also a great way to get out of the house, make new friends, and create new experiences. There are many types of volunteering; the first step is to build it into your schedule.

Schedule It

Things come up for all of us, and many times volunteering is the first thing to be forgotten when your schedule gets tight. Yet, volunteering should be part of your weekly or monthly duties. It is something that is not done to mark off a checklist but rather with the intention of helping and giving. Your intention plays a large role in volunteering. You are not wasting your time and there are no other things you could be doing. You are there to give the best of yourself to a cause that may not benefit you directly. However, indirectly you will gain so much by volunteering.

Building Relationships

You will build relationships; some of which will extend beyond volunteering and prove long lasting. The building of relationships comes again to attitude. While volunteering, have an attitude of helping others. Be conscious of your thoughts as they are often visible on your face and in your body language. And as we all know, body language communicates much more than our words. This is something to always remember as you leave your home.

As stated in the previous chapter, your attitude must be checked at the door. Once you leave your home, your attitude should be welcoming of others. A welcoming attitude shows on your smile, in your walk, and throughout your laughter. This attitude will create great experiences and relationships. As you take on this warm, kind, and open attitude others with similar attitudes will draw to you. This is your crowd. These individuals with a similar interest and a similar attitude are the people who will form your circle of friends.

Part of the Veteran's Nature

Volunteering comes easy for most veterans as it is in our nature of service. This is a prime example of bringing the best of the military culture to the general population. This blending gives the veteran an edge throughout his or her life. The hardest part is being committed enough to schedule volunteering in your calendar and actually showing up.

Volunteering also provides a sense of purpose or additional purpose. As you become a regular face at a chosen volunteer organization, you will begin realizing the importance of showing up: others need and depend on you. For a personal gain, volunteering diminishes anxiety and other adjustment disorders. The social contact, along with meditation, reflection, and keeping a journal will assist the veteran in his adjustment process.

Working

Not to be overlooked, working also creates new experiences for veterans. This is a practical and conventional arena for gaining experience, meeting new people, and developing as a person. Veterans are favored in many job positions because of the blend of military and civilian culture.

Teamwork and Leadership

Veterans are considered by many employers to be better at teamwork. This is an obvious byproduct of our years working in teams in the military. In addition to team work, veterans are also better leaders as compared to their age group. A 22 year old sergeant who has led a squad during combat missions will have exponentially more leadership skills than his counterparts in the general population.

Translate Your Resume

Although employers seek veterans to fill their ranks, veterans many times have a hard time showing that they are qualified. The veteran resume is usually filled with military jargon that many simply do not understand. Transferring military experience into a civilian resume leaves many veterans behind. Books at your local library and online tutorials are best when preparing resumes. This resume preparation can mean the difference between having the management job you are qualified for and being hired at the entry level.

Education

In addition to being a veteran, many employers will also look for education level as well. The different educational benefits are in place for veterans transitioning to the general population. If eligible for educational benefits, a veteran should strongly consider going to college. It has been made easier as a living allowance is now available for the majority of veterans (Post 9-11 GI Bill). There are now even less excuses for not going to college.

Advantages in School

Veterans have an advantage in school that is similar to the workplace. Veterans are great leaders and our experience creates a great learning environment for all students within the class. Many veterans are also more organized than others their age. This organization has been indoctrinated in us through years of accountability and responsibility. Veterans are usually on time with their priorities well in order.

While many students may want to experience the nightlife and party scene, veterans are usually focused on their goal: obtaining the degree. Many veterans are focused because we have seen the work environment and many of us better understand the requirements for our position of choice. We are students with purpose and the nightlife is not new to us. Many veterans also have families. Families provide that extra motivation to succeed and provide for your home. Partying and club-hopping is done modestly if at all.

The advantages to being a veteran are noticed by employers and school faculty alike. This advantage is the determination and willingness that most veterans display. It is also the experience level that veterans hold over the majority within the general population.

Summary

Enjoying life may be a forceful drag at first. But it will soon turn into effortless love. The video games, movies, and computer can wait. Your life is here and it must takes priority. The smells of the city, the rising sun over a horizon, and the awesome people you meet each day cannot wait.

A great way to meet people and serve is volunteering. Volunteering is in the nature of the veteran. Volunteering brings benefit not only for the cause but also for you; anxiety and other disorders are diminished by the social contact.

Two other ways to make new experiences is through the workplace and school. Both employers and school faculty value veterans and our contributions. Employers enjoy our teamwork mindset, our leadership, and our experience. Veterans have an advantage in the university based on our experience, our determination to succeed, and our organization. It is our determination to succeed that drives many of us to success both in the workplace and the university. Similar to exercising or adopting a healthier diet, determination is so often the key.

8
Triggers

No Object Is Sacrosanct

'Change is difficult but often essential to survival'

– Les Brown

Various Types

The triggers are present in many of our lives. They come from a variety of sources and cause any number of negative effects in our lives. The first rule in dealing with triggers is a simple one, if something causes discomfort, let it go! Now, this 'something' could also be written as 'someone' or 'some scenario'. This includes friends, family, threatening areas, uncomfortable bar and nightlife areas, rowdy people, and sensory triggers.

Dealing with Triggers

Many within the above list may cause discomfort appearing in the form of anger, anxiety, or depression. A person or situation can play the role of a trigger and bring discomfort or stagnation to the adjustment process. Most triggers are easily avoided or deleted from your life. Family and friends are not always as easy to distance yourself from, yet sometimes this measure is necessary. This does not mean that if your wife yells every other day to rush and file for a divorce. Let us not cut off our noses to spite our face. Be rational.

Communication

However, if the trigger is a valuable person in your life, such as a spouse, family member, or important friend you must explain to the person the harm they are causing in your adjustment process. This can be difficult as it exposes the vulnerability of recovery. It brings your personal issues to light. Many veterans choose silence as the best method of communication. But life does not work that way. Communication is a far greater tool than silence, distance, or the combination of both. If this is too great a task to hurdle, remember your journal that you have been keeping. This will track your progress from the beginning of your self-help to the present.

As we saw in the fourth chapter, a journal is a great communica-tion tool and will allow the reader to glimpse into your behavior and thoughts. They will see the improvement in both. And depending on if you mentioned them in the journal, they will also see the pain or agitation that they are causing.

This adds additional importance on keeping the journal objective and accurate. A biased journal will cause more strain to the relation-ship than good. Journal the event fairly and paint yourself in an accu-rate and honest manner. Once they view the journal, they will see the specific incidences that have bothered you. They will benefit in exactly the same way that you benefit from the journal; they will see their actions in an objective manner.

At this point they can decide to work with you in establishing a healthier relationship or to continue to be your antagonist. Many will be more conscious of how they interact with you, some have sympa-thy for you, and others will simply not care. Only the first group is satisfactory.

You want individuals to be conscious in their behavior like you are, but you do not want a horde of people feeling sorry for you. Their empathy is welcomed but the sympathy is not necessary. You are not a victim. You are a veteran adjusting to the general population. There is a difference. The last group needs little explanation. The individuals who refuse to acknowledge their actions should be kept at a distance.

Strengthening Relationships

If they are now working with you, your relationship with one another has grown. Whether the antagonist is your spouse, parent, sibling, coworker, or friend, once they reach the point of choosing to assist in your adjustment process rather than obstructing it they become closer. These are the friends and family members who strengthen you. They are not feeling sorry for you, but instead they are there to help. They are there to listen to you and honor your journey. Strengthening a relationship can be a special moment for both parties. Do not forget to journal.

Removing Triggers

If they express a lack of empathy for your adjustment process then you must take action. This action does not consist of meeting fire with fire and beginning an argument. Instead, you must remove yourself from the relationship for a couple of days to form the smartest decision. Only after this break should you make a decision on the relationship. Avoid making hasty decisions formed over emotions. This is an easy mistake to make. Once you open up to someone and they disregard, you or even use your vulnerability against you, it is easy to find yourself enraged and participating in a yelling match.

Before you begin this madness and bring yourself to a new low, say to yourself 'Is this person worthy of my sanity?' The answer to that question will always be 'NO!' *Emphatically NO!* There neither exists nor will there ever exist a person worthy of your sanity. You must take care of yourself first or you will not have anything to give to anyone else. The best scenario is simply to walk away and keep your sanity and dignity intact. Value your sanity and let the stubborn person go.

Trigger as an Object

A trigger can be anything that causes depression, anxiety, paranoia, sadness, flashbacks, nightmares, automatic anger, or day-mares. If a trigger is an inanimate object, it is much easier to suppress than a person. You do not have to explain your situation to an object, and you do not have to show it your journal in hopes that it will consider your process and change its behaviors. It will not have its own opinion of several different events and it will not look to win in an argument. When a trigger is an object, you simply have to cut it out of your life.

When in Doubt, Throw it Out

When considering objects to eject out of your life, leave no stone unturned in your searching efforts. When in doubt throw it out! It is best to remove one too many things than to keep a couple around that bring you back to the discomfort. Everything is up for evaluation. Be sure to track discomforts in your journal to make the process of locating triggers easier.

Only Your Sanity is Sacrosanct

Inanimate triggers come in a variety of forms including sitcoms, songs, military uniforms and awards, smells, foods, pictures, and fireworks. Remember, no object is sacrosanct. You must look at the situation as an objective statement: either this trigger or my sanity has to go. I am sure you will make the right decision.

Determination over the Trigger

Some triggers such as songs, personal war photos, and foods are easily avoided and thrown out of your life. You control each of these triggers and their involvement in your life. Other triggers, such as fireworks and heavy exhaust fumes are not totally in your control. Generally, your environment controls these triggers. Therefore, you must enact mind over matter until the situation leaves; or you must leave the situation.

Uncontrolled triggers will empower your determination if you stick the situation out. As the fumes begin causing flashbacks of Baghdad, choose to be where you are. Choose not to have that flashback. As soon as you realize you are having the flashback, force yourself to end it. If you are having a hard time keeping the discomfort out, then avoiding the trigger is the only intelligent option left.

Fireworks

Many combat veterans have flashbacks or feeling of unease when they hear fireworks. Some of the fireworks sound like an ambush when you do not expect them, while others, known as salutes, mimic mortar and artillery shelling. For a veteran, especially a combat veteran, small arms fire and an incoming bombardment can be reasons to panic not celebrate. It is common to see veterans take cover as a second nature survival tool until they realize that the blasts are in the name of festive fun.

Another trigger stemming from the use of fireworks is the aftermath smell. The gunpowder scent can conjure up the most detailed flashbacks.

Cultural Norm

Most people using fireworks are obviously not doing it to give veterans flashbacks, but sometimes they are blatantly inconsiderate. Instead of going to a park on a designated day, or congregating at a large, beautiful, spectacular, and planned firework display, many celebrants ignite fireworks in residential neighborhoods without any warning. Most people simply do not understand how random, small arms fire sounding fireworks affect their veteran neighbors. In this situation, check with local laws regarding fireworks. In many areas, fireworks are illegal in residential neighborhoods. Some even go so far as to state that they are illegal on Independence Day.

Understand the Law

I am not advocating calling the police on every kid with a cherry bomb; however, when you understand the law you can handle the situation better. The best option is to talk with the people igniting the fireworks. If their fireworks are indeed illegal in residential neighborhoods, relay that to them. If they are young, you may prefer talking with their parents or guardians.

The Law shall Prevail

If they stop great but do not expect it. Most are very enthusiastic about their firework display and see an objection as anti-American. Many have come to see fireworks as a patriotic symbol of freedom and independence. Some may also provide a patriotic speech where they explain the importance of fireworks for the countries identity. But the law is the law, and if they do not stop they are willingly breaking it. At this stage it comes back to that objective statement covered earlier: either this trigger or my sanity has to go. You have done your best to inform them about the laws, now they can receive their next warning from the police.

Determination over Fireworks

Remember there is also another option. That is the option of not letting the discomfort in. Being aware of the discomfort and using determination to keep it out. You know that the fireworks are going to last the entire night so you build a barrier against it. Keep the discomfort out.

Legal

If you are living in an area where fireworks are legal in residential areas then your options are obviously limited. You still have the choice to explain your discomfort with the antagonist. But if they disregard your adjustment process then there is little left for you to do to stop them.

You could however, try to drown out the noise by playing music loudly. These are times when meditation may also provide comfort in a time of discomfort. Meditate to control your emotions, automatic reactions, and suppress any anxiety. Just know that discomfort brought by triggers cannot last forever. In addition, remember to not let this discomfort in. This will prove useful to veterans with many seemingly uncontrollable triggers. It is also a sure way to be comfortable and in control at all times.

STORY – Beautiful Uniform with Unnerving Affects

For a Marine, his trigger came in the form of an old uniform. This Marine kept his dress blue uniform neatly pressed in his closet. It had been there for the past two years since his discharge from the military. The uniform, decorated with medals and ribbons, hung among other regularly used clothing. This uniform hung for him to see each and every day. As he dressed himself in the morning, there was the uniform.

For some, it would seem bizarre to have an old uniform hanging with suits. Yet what was more puzzling were the affects the uniform created. What began with the intention of prideful remembrance became a painful discomfort.

This uniform began causing flashbacks and anxiety within a few months after his discharge. He remembered past friends and past events. He remembered his unit, the firefights they experienced, and the smells associated with battle. After the anxiety and frequent flashbacks, the uniform still hung there for him to see.

The solution for this case was simple: remove the uniform. Remember the mantra: either this trigger or my sanity has to go. This veteran had a few options. He could have thrown the uniforms away, he could have boxed it up and forgotten about it, or he could have left it where it was and suffer from anxiety and flashbacks for the remainder of his life. The veteran's choice was a good one. He boxed up the uniform, the medals, and the certificates and sent them to his mother. Out of sight, out of mind! This was a great, yet temporary approach. Once he has adjusted fully, he can send for his uniform and awards. But in the meantime, there is one less trigger causing him ill effects.

In addition, it is important to not only remove a trigger but to also concentrate on the automatic emotions that it draws out of you. No inanimate object should have any power over you. No uniform should cause stress, no exhaust smoke should cause flashbacks, and

no fireworks should create anxiety. Here, we must look back to meditation and reflection.

Meditation will allow us to better control our emotions and
defuse anger and anxiety. Some triggers cause an instant depression as you remember past events; meditation works here too. The
depression that many veterans experience can quickly move away
with meditation and reflection.

Reflection is important to take the flashbacks that triggers cause
and address them objectively. Triggers highlight areas that need to
be focused on. Many flashbacks are things that we have failed to
address. Triggers add purpose and meaning to meditation and reflection. In this manner, we can thank the trigger before releasing it.

STORY end

Identify the Solution

Here we see that triggers are usually glaringly obvious. Sometimes
however, they are subtle. Rather they are easily noticed or less apparent; find them and their solution at the same time. The solution is
very important in removing the trigger from our lives. It is not good
enough to simply identify the areas that make us tick; we have to
identify the solution so we can target and neutralize them.

Act on Solutions

All triggers have a solution. Some solutions do not seem practical and
many will work better for some veterans than others. When a solution does not seem practical, usually because a person believes that
he needs a certain trigger, remember the mantra that clearly states
that your sanity is not to be compromised. If all options have been
exhausted, then you must make the tougher decision. This tougher
decision may include ending a relationship, throwing away your old

uniform, and relocating to a new area. In each case, the decision will be a good one if it increases the quality of your life.

Culture Shocks

There have been a few triggers that stood in the way between whom I was and whom I wished to become. I, like many combat veterans, experienced these triggers during two key transitions: from combat to garrison and from garrison to the general population. Both instances can be a culture shock. The combat veteran must adjust to a slower life in the garrison army and the veteran must reacclimate to the general population.

Depending on the veteran, one adjustment phase will be more difficult than others. Yet for many, the adjustment to the general population presents more challenges. However, both are important chapters in the life of a veteran.

The Form of a Trigger Depends on the Veteran

The triggers that many veterans experience are not always immediately noticeable. Some are attached to tangible objects and others to intangible objects depending on a veteran's mood. For many veterans, if they are depressed, or especially reflective on a perceived negative event, an object may trigger a chain of responses associated with that event. It could be a song heard for the entire week without any ill effects. Suddenly, or so it seems, hearing this song would create anxiety and flashbacks simultaneously.

Growing Pains are Normal

Other triggers latch on to objects, tangible and intangible, with striking consistency. For me, the trigger was war pictures. Upon returning home from Iraq, I experienced a few adjustment disorders. But looking back at fellow veterans, my adjustment process was normal. A veteran returning from a combat zone or returning to the general population should expect some growing pains.

As we move from one distinct culture to another, certain areas of our lives snag behind. This is a culture shock at its best; or worst. Normally a culture shock is attached to the experience of a world traveler; an Iowan farmer being dropped off in the bustling city of Johannesburg. However, there are other culture shocks that are created by leaving a culture then returning to it at a different stage in your life. Things can seem foreign in these situations.

Many Prisoners Experience Culture Shock

A freed prisoner is a prime and great example of a culture shock. This person may have been a misfit prior to being incarcerated, to however great a degree, but when he returns to society after a long period of imprisonment he may experience a cultural shock. These individuals are placed into the same community that they left yet a culture shock is created and experienced because the community and the person have changed. This phenomenon is captured in part by the recidivism rate. For the United States, the current recidivism rate is well over 60%.

The principles in this book will not only help veterans, but will help prisoners as well. Both veterans and prisoners have complained that they were ill prepared for the reality of the general population. The veteran holds obvious advantages over the ex-prisoner, yet both are coming into a general population different from where they came. Both are experiencing growing pains. The purpose of this book is not to avoid these growing pains but rather to guide the veteran to self-improvement.

My Trigger

During my adjustment process, a major road-blocking trigger was given to me from a good friend: pictures. War pictures. This friend downloaded over 600 pictures from our tour in Iraq. The pictures were not too gory;

there were no pictures of dead bodies or severely hurt people. There were however pictures of individuals who would later be killed in action. There were also snapshots of significant areas; areas that drew instant flashbacks and smells. These were significant areas where blood was shed, where we huddled in the cold, where we hurried up and waited, and places where we shared meals. These were significant pictures that told an awesome story. The words leaped from the photos.

Memories Caused Nightmares

Soon after viewing each picture, I began remembering the details of combat that I had conveniently forgotten. Eventually, the memories were replaced by nightmares. Instead of seeing friends and areas, I saw war and the worst of it. I saw the pain, the frustration of fighting a faceless enemy in an unconventional war. Day after day of sleep reducing nightmares forced me to make a decision. There seemed to be only one responsible decision: delete all of the digital photos from my computer. They served no constructive purpose.

The Mantra

Prior to deleting these pictures, I developed the mantra for triggers: either this trigger or my sanity has to go. After ridding myself of these pictures, I began to examine my life, looking for more triggers that would hinder my adjustment process.

For many, photos will not be a trigger. Many celebrate the pictures and use it as a calming tool. They remember their younger days with pleasure. Many of my veteran buddies would huddle around one computer and provide caption for each picture. This was always a fun event that created explosive debates; guys giving their opinions of past action. Those debates became heated arguments fast, yet the cheerfulness was still there as the foundation of the discussion.

A week after the photos were deleted, the recurring nightmares were gone. They were only memories. From that moment, I understood that my external triggers could be successfully targeted and neutralized. I realized that nothing that causes me discomfort is sacrosanct. No object, tangible or not, is worth my sanity. From this time, I began taking a fine tooth comb over my life and started to critically evaluate each element of my life.

Highlight, Problem, and Solution

I also took this time to refocus on meditation and reflection. It was not enough to delete the pictures. I had to target the reaction and not the object. The reaction was the problem, and the trigger was only the noticeable highlight. The solution is behind the problem and *not* the trigger. The trigger allows us to see where we need to focus. It gives us direction and it humbles us.

Reflection was an essential component in my adjustment process. It was necessary to reduce the reactions hovering around objects. The trigger provided the problem. The problem was nightmares of past events; events tied to sympathy and anxiety. Once I targeted the events and reflected on them objectively, the problem fell away. These nightmares never returned.

Throughout the process I chose to journal the adjustment process. It began as a way to analyze nightmares but evolved into a diary of adjustment. Soon the entries made were tracked and compared with months earlier. The journal became a great recording tool into my mind of yesterday. It communicated to me about my forgotten inner thoughts. Thoughts and behaviors jotted down months prior was compiled and contrasted with the current counterparts. It aided in development, confidence, and a speedy adjustment process.

Aware of Your Surroundings

Sometimes it is necessary to not only avoid objects but also to avoid situations. For many veteran party-goers, the club tough guy is a constant threat to a successful adjustment process. This club tough guy drinks and yells aggressively. Along with a drinking veteran, this combination may prove explosive.

A joke taken out of context, refusal to appreciate a veteran's service, or any number of minor incidences can spur into a verbal or physical battle. Controlling the external environment is never a guarantee. You have little control over the characters that you come into contact with on a daily basis. And they have little control over you and your behavior.

External and Internal Environments

Under the influence of alcohol, it is not only the external environment that is out of your control but also your internal environment. A single drunk night of verbal sparring with the club's resident tough guy can set back weeks of improvement. And the effects thereafter can be long lasting as you replay the sequence of events and go through the 'If I see him again' scenarios. This is just more things to work through in your adjustment process.

Remember the Mantra

Obviously, the best situation is to avoid the environment until your adjustment is complete. For many night owls, avoiding the club scene may prove difficult to impossible as they label the alternative as a dull or boring life. But at this point, remember the mantra that states it is either this trigger or my sanity. One of these two, sanity or trigger, has to leave because there is not enough room for both.

Friends

Friends also help at these times. Enjoying the company of friends is an excellent way to control your external environment. If you are still conquering alcoholism, drink at home or at gatherings with trusted friends. Your friends will push you in the right direction. These friends will tell you when enough is enough as opposed to encouraging you to take another round of the beer bong. This adds importance in choosing quality individuals as friends.

While inebriated, there will be no quality time to concern yourself with the friends around you. As stated in chapter six, concentrating on improving yourself will also improve your crowd of friends. Some will grow with you and others will leave your crowd and gradually fall from communication. The right crowd will assist you in your growth as opposed to feeding your addictions and vices for a laugh or a display of machismo. The foundation to improving your crowd is improving yourself.

Summary

Triggers affect the lives of many veterans. They come in a variety of forms and cause a number of effects. Triggers are identified as part of the adjustment process that is a norm for veterans. This adjustment process can be broken down into two types. First is the combat veteran's adjustment from warfare to garrison and the second is the veteran's adjustment from garrison to the general population. In both types, triggers can affect the process.

The mantra for triggers, it is either this trigger or my sanity, is used to bring the trigger into perspective. This trigger may be a family member, an old friend, a picture, or a smell. Regardless of its form, each trigger must be removed. This can become tricky for an annoying and argumentative loved one. Here, you should explain your process in hopes that the antagonist will become more understanding. However, if he is still annoying and unempathetic you should distance yourself for a time. If the family member or friend becomes more conscious of his behavior, then the relationship can flourish to a new height.

In addition to making stronger relationships with loved ones, triggers will allow you to focus on key areas in your adjustment process. The trigger will highlight a problem such as anxiety or anger.